# Alfred Nobel

## An Extraordinary Man
## Behind Nobel Prize

**MRS. SONALI DORGE-PHULE**

ISBN:9798640364804

# DEDICATION


Dear Aaradhya,
You are such a kindhearted girl! Your shining smile, endless energy… There is no one like you in the whole world! I am so proud of you. You can do anything you set in your mind. Never stop reaching for your dreams, keep questioning, learning, and discovering. Whenever you need a reminder of how amazing you are, just open this book and remember that I love you always.

# TABLE OF CONTENTS

# ACKNOWLEDGMENT

Writing a book series is much harder than I thought
and more rewarding than I could have ever imagined.
"I want to thank my lovable husband Dr. Ajit, Thank you dear!
You never stopped me; only encouraged me."
I recognized and acknowledged you, the reader!!
Thank you so much!!!

# ALFRED NOBEL

Alfred Nobel

Immanuel Nobel
(Father of Alfred Nobel)

Andriette Nobel
(Mother of Alfred Nobel)

On October 21, 1833, a baby boy was born to a family in Stockholm, Sweden, who was to become a famous scientist, inventor, businessman, and founder of the Nobel Prizes. His father was Immanuel Nobel and his mother was Andriette Ahlsell Nobel. They named their son Alfred.

Nobel was fluent in several languages and wrote poetry as well as drama. Nobel was also very interested in social and peace-related issues and held views that were considered radical during his time. Alfred Nobel's interests are reflected in the prize which he established.

Alfred had two older brothers, Robert born in 1829, and Ludvig born in 1831. Alfred's father was an engineer and inventor. He built bridges and buildings and experimented with different ways of blasting rocks. The same year that Alfred was born, his father's business suffered losses and had to be closed. In 1837, Immanuel Nobel decided to try his business somewhere else and left for Finland and Russia. Alfred's mother was left behind in Stockholm to take care of the family. Andriette Nobel, who came from a wealthy family, started a grocery store. The store had a modest income that helped in supporting the family.

After a time, Immanuel Nobel's business in St. Petersburg, Russia started doing well. He had opened a mechanical workshop that provided equipment for the Russian army. He also made the Russian Tsar and his generals believe that sea mines could be used to stop enemy ships from entering and attacking St. Petersburg. The mines stopped the British Royal Navy from moving into firing range of St. Petersburg during the Crimean war in 1853-1856. The naval mines designed by Immanuel Nobel were simple devices consisting of submerged wooden casks filled with gunpowder. Immanuel Nobel was also a pioneer in arms manufacture and in designing steam engines.

With his success in Russia, Immanuel was now able to move his family to St. Petersburg in 1842. By 1843, another boy was born into the family, Emil. The four Nobel brothers were given first class education with the help of private tutors. Their lessons included natural sciences, languages, and literature. At the age of 17, Alfred could speak and write various languages including Swedish, Russian, French, English, and German. Robert and Ludvig became engineers, while Alfred studied chemistry.

The Nobel brothers (clockwise) Robert, Alfred, Ludvig and baby Emil. This photo is from St. Petersburg, around 1843.

Alfred was most interested in literature, chemistry, and physics. However, Alfred Nobel's interest in philosophy started early with the great philosophers, from Plato and Aristotle onward. While still in St. Petersburg he improved his French by translating Voltaire into Swedish and then back into French; after which he would compare the final version with the French original. To increase his vocabulary, he memorized dictionaries page after page, perhaps to compensate for his weak physical powers. At the age of 18, Alfred wrote a first version of an autobiographical poem of 425 lines in excellent English – "You say I am a riddle" – that gives an indication of his life and thoughts during the years of his-- otherwise little-known childhood and early youth. His father wanted his sons to follow his footsteps and was not pleased with Alfred's interest in poetry. He decided to send the young man abroad to study and become a chemical engineer.

Alfred Nobel neither attended any university nor perceived any degree. His tutorial instruction came to an end as early as 1850. In Paris, at the recommendation of his chemistry teacher, Professor Zinin – Alfred worked in the private laboratory of Professor T. J. Pelouze, a famous chemist. There, he met a young Italian chemist, Ascanio Sobrero. Three years earlier, Sobrero had invented nitro-glycerine, a highly explosive liquid. Nitro-glycerine was produced by mixing glycerine with sulfuric and nitric acid. Nitro-glycerine possessed violent explosive power, but no one had devised a solution regarding how to control this highly dangerous substance.

Alfred became very interested in nitro-glycerine and how it could be used in construction work. He also realized that the safety problems had to be solved and a method had to be developed for the controlled detonation of nitro-glycerine. When he returned to Russia after his studies, he worked together with his father to develop nitro-glycerine as a commercially and technically useful explosive.

After the Crimean War ended, the business of Alfred's father went badly, and he decided to move back to Sweden. Alfred's elder brothers Robert and Ludvig stayed in Russia to try and save the remaining family business. They became successful and went on to develop the oil industry in the southern part of Russia. They were very successful and became some of the wealthiest persons of their time.

Immanuel and two of his sons, Alfred, and Emil return to Sweden. Alfred focused on developing nitro-glycerine as an explosive. Unfortunately, these experiments resulted in accidents that killed several people, including Alfred's younger brother, Emil. The government decided to ban these experiments within the Stockholm city limits. Alfred did not give up and moved his experiments to a barge or flat bottom boat on Lake Malaren. In 1864, he was able to start mass production of nitro-glycerine, but he did not stop experimenting with different additives to make the production much safer.

## Invention of Dynamite

Alfred also continued the nitro-glycerine explosive experiments begun by his father, first working alone in St. Petersburg and later together with his father in Stockholm. The approaches which have been resulted by Immanuel was completely wrong. With his father's failure in mind, Alfred tried entirely different methods for using nitro-glycerine as an explosive. To make the handling of nitro-glycerine safer, Alfred Nobel experimented with different additives. Alfred found through his experiments, that mixing nitro-glycerine with a fine sand called *kieselguhr* would turn the liquid into paste which could be shaped into rods. These rods could then be inserted into drilling holes. The invention was made in 1866. Alfred got a patent, or legal right of ownership on this material the next year. He named it "dynamite." He also invented a detonator or blasting cap which could be set off by lighting a fuse. Inventions were made at a time when the diamond drilling crown and pneumatic drill came into general use. Together, these inventions helped reduce the cost of many construction work like drilling tunnels, blasting rocks, building bridges, etc.

Alfred Nobel's laboratory in Bofors, Sweden.

The market for dynamite and detonating caps grew very rapidly and Alfred Nobel also proved himself to be a very skillful entrepreneur and businessman. Because of this success, Alfred was able to put up factories in 90 different places. He lived in Paris but often travelled to his factories in more than 20 countries. He was once described as "Europe's richest vagabond." He worked intensively in Stockholm (Sweden), Hamburg (Germany), Ardeer (Scotland), Paris and Sevran (France), Karlskoga (Sweden) and San Remo (Italy). He also did experiments to make synthetic rubber and leather and artificial silk. He had 355 patents by the time of his death in 1896. Alfred Nobel never had his own dynamite factory in Russia. Nevertheless, a large share of Alfred Nobel's fortune came from his investments in Russia. He never expressed his real feelings about that country.

Intensive work and travel did not leave much time for his private life. At the age of 43 he was feeling like an old man. Alfred had no family of his own. One day, he announced in the newspapers for a secretary and supervisor of household. An Austrian lady, Bertha Kinsky von Chinic und Tettau got the job. After working for a short time, she moved back to Austria to marry Count Arthur von Suttner.

Alfred and Bertha von Suttner remained friends and exchanged their letters through the years. She later became very active in the peace movement. She wrote the famous book "Lay Down Your Arms." When Alfred Nobel later wrote his will to establish the Nobel Prizes, he included a prize for persons or organizations who promoted peace. Several years after the death of Alfred Nobel, the Norwegian Storting (Parliament) decided to award the 1905 Nobel Peace Prize to Bertha von Suttner.

Many of the companies founded by Nobel have developed into industrial enterprises that still play a prominent role in the world economy, for example Imperial Chemical Industries (ICI), Great Britain; Société Centrale de Dynamite, France; and Dyno Industries in Norway. Toward the end of his life, he acquired the company AB Bofors in Karlskoga, where Björkborn Manor became his Swedish home.

During most of his life, Alfred Nobel suffered from poor health. He complained of indigestion, headaches, and occasional spells of depression. Already as a young man, he spent several weeks at health resorts. His first stay at a spa was at Franzenbad in Bohemia in 1854. The inactivity at the health resorts made him restless and bored. He cannot have been impressed by the medical treatment offered at the spas. It consisted of baths, resting, and drinking well water. Toward the end of his life, Alfred Nobel suffered from a heart condition marked by paroxysms of intense pain (angina pectoris). The real nature of his health problems at a younger age are not clear, but one may well imagine that he was simply overworked or under serious mental stress. Often, he felt lonely and without friends. He spent long hours in the laboratory working with toxic chemicals under primitive conditions. In addition to the laboratory work, Nobel handled his correspondence with factories, banks, and collaborators all by himself. He travelled a lot and did not have a home.

Explosions in his factories, sometimes with many casualties, the resulting bad publicity, as well as patent infringements and the legal procedures to protect his patents, added to his burden. The 80's and early 90's, was a period of frequent depressions but, despite this, he showed great tenacity and carried on with his work. Toward his final years, he was in a more cheerful mood and planned to reduce his personal engagement in business activity and to return to Sweden. Finally, he suffered a stroke, was partly paralyzed, and died at San Remo at 2:00 a.m. on December 10, 1896. In his last will and testament, he wrote that much of his fortune was to be used to give prizes to those who have done their best for humanity in the field of physics, chemistry, physiology or medicine, literature, and peace. Not everybody was pleased with this. His will was opposed by his relatives and questioned by authorities in various countries. It took four years for his executors to convince all parties to follow Alfred's wishes. The executors of his will were two young engineers, Ragnar Sohlman and Rudolf Lilljequist. They set about forming the Nobel Foundation as an organization to take care of the financial assets left by Nobel for this purpose and to coordinate the work of the Prize-Awarding Institutions.

In 1901, the first Nobel Prizes in Physics, Chemistry, Physiology or Medicine and Literature were first awarded in Stockholm, Sweden, and the Peace Prize in Kristiania (now Oslo), Norway.

# INTEREST IN MEDICINE

In his will Alfred Nobel specified that the bulk of his estate should be deposited in a fund, the interest of which should be divided into five parts and to be used for Prizes in Physics, Chemistry, Literature and Peace. One of the five shares should be given to the person "who shall have made the most important discovery within the domain of Physiology or Medicine"

What motivated Alfred Nobel to specify a prize in physiology or medicine? Was it because of his own health problems or was he genuinely interested in scientific problems in these areas?

Why did he choose the Royal Caroline Medico-Surgical Institute at a time when there were older and more established medical faculties at the universities of Uppsala and Lund? Did he have personal contacts with the Institute? How did the Institute respond to the will and the task of awarding the Nobel Prize in Physiology or Medicine? Did he make any other donations to medical research?

Alfred Nobel's interest in physiology and medicine was genuinely scientific. In his laboratory notebooks, he often made notes about ideas that should be tested "to mitigate or cure disease". He was interested in anaesthesia and listed substances and alcohols that might be useful for this purpose. He also contemplated intravenous injection of anaesthetic agents as an alternative to the ether and chloroform anaesthesia that was commonly used at his time.

The discoverer of nitro-glycerine, Ascanio Sobrero, had noted at that time, that exposure to this chemical may cause severe headaches. Alfred Nobel, who spent much of his time experimenting with this substance, must have had experienced this effect and later on, when nitro-glycerine was produced at an industrial level, it is reasonable to assume that nitro-glycerine was a serious medical and environmental problem, also for his collaborators. On the other hand, in some situations, nitro-glycerine is useful in the treatment of disease. Lauder Brunton, a distinguished British physician, had found in 1867 that organic nitrates were effective in relieving pains in angina pectoris. When in 1890 Nobel's physicians recommended nitro-glycerine as a remedy for his heart disease, he declined it.

Nitro-glycerine has now been used in the treatment of angina pectoris for more than 100 years without anyone knowing its physiological mechanism of action. Thanks to the work of Robert Furchgott, Louis Ignarro, and Ferid Murad, who share the1998 Nobel Prize in Physiology or Medicine, we now know that nitro-glycerine acts by releasing nitric oxide, NO, a common gas and environmental pollutant. The gas is released in the endothelial cell layer lining the interior surface of blood vessels. From there, it diffuses into the smooth muscle cell layer, triggering a relaxation of its myofilaments. As a result, the blood vessel widens allowing more blood to pass. The improved circulation means more oxygen for the heart muscle and the pain is reduced.

Alfred Nobel had personal contacts with representatives of the Karolinska Institute. One of them was Dr. Sten von Hofsten, a paediatrician and assistant professor at the Karolinska Institute, who assisted in arranging a fund honouring his mother. Hofsten was surprised at Alfred Nobel's interest in biology and physiology, and they had long discussions on both subjects.

In 1890, von Hofsten met with Alfred Nobel in Paris and found that the latter had a genuine interest in the medical sciences. Nobel expressed his wish to become acquainted with some young, well-trained Swedish physiologist with whom he could work, or rather who might be able to carry out some of the many original and ingenious ideas on the subject of physiology that were germinating in his highly inventive brain. Through the mediation of von Hofsten, Johan Erik (Jöns) Johansson was invited to work on blood transfusion at Alfred Nobel's laboratory at Sevran outside Paris. Johansson accepted the invitation and spent 5 months in Sevran. In Alfred Nobel's view, the main difficulties with blood transfusion was that blood changes very rapidly outside the body and that blood, therefore, had to be directly transferred from the donor to the recipient. Tubings made of molten borax and sodium were particularly suited for such transfers since they would cause minimum damage to the blood corpuscles. This, of course, was before the problem of blood groups had been solved and nothing came of these ideas.

When Alfred Nobel's will was opened in 1896, it was questioned by some of his relatives. Its exact wording was subjected to detailed analysis when the statutes of the Nobel Foundation were written. The Royal Caroline Medico-Surgical Institute was represented by its rector, Count Mörner. Within the faculty the opinion was divided. Some members hesitated in getting the Institute involved if the claims of the relatives had not been settled. Jöns Johansson, now professor at Karolinska Institute, took an active part in the faculty work. Being the only person on the faculty who had worked with Alfred Nobel and knowing his interests in medicine, he played an important role in formulating the final rules. After some deliberations and compromises, "the domain of physiology or medicine" was understood to encompass the theoretical as well as the practical medical sciences. This left the prize-awarding institution considerable freedom in making its own interpretation. Over the years, awards have been made both to the theoretical and preclinical sciences, as well as to clinical medicine.

In fact, the interpretation has been liberal and has included topics ranging from behavioural sciences to plant genetics.

The donation made in the will was not the first that Alfred Nobel made to medical research. In 1890 he donated SEK 50,000 to the Royal Caroline Medico-Surgical Institute in order to create a fund in the memory of his mother Andriette Nobel. The aim of the fund was to promote experimental research "in all branches of medical science and to facilitate using the fruits of such research in teaching as well as in medical literature."

Alfred Nobel also supported medical research in Russia where he grew up and studied with private tutors. Sometime around 1894 the Russian physiologist I.P. Pavlov and M. Nencki, professor of medical chemistry at St. Petersburg received financial support for their experimental work.

# INTEREST IN LITERATURE

During his lifetime, Alfred Nobel was undoubtedly more renowned for his work as an inventor and industrialist than for his interests in the arts. However, to understand his versatility, his complex and at times contradictory nature, these interests that were also vital to him must be considered as well.

Although Nobel belonged to the realm of his work and inventions, his second home was in literature and writing. After his death he left a private library of over 1500 volumes, mostly fiction in the original language, works by the great writers of the 19th century, but also the classics and works by philosophers, theologians, historians, and other scientists.

He also left a voluminous collection of letters, a handful of poems he himself had written in his youth and some early drafts of analytical novels, *I ljusaste Afrika* (In Brightest Africa, 1861) and *Systrarna* (The Sisters, 1862). Towards the end of his life, when his inventions and business activities left him more time, he drafted the outline of a satirical comedy, *The Patent Bacillus* (1895), and published a tragedy, *Nemesis* (1896). Nobel's will, dated 1895, is the final testimony to his lifelong love of poetry: one of the prizes was to be awarded to "the person who shall have produced in the field of literature the most outstanding work in an ideal direction".

During his education in St. Petersburg, Alfred Nobel was taught by outstanding private tutors, mainly chemistry and physics, but also literature and philosophy. He proved to be a precocious pupil, exceptionally gifted, but quiet and introvert. He learnt a great deal on his own – French by translating Voltaire, first into Swedish and then back into French and checking it against the original. He read the *Odyssey,* Pushkin's verse epic *Eugene Onegin* and *Home of the Gentry* by Turgenev in Russian. At the age of 17, he was not only fluent in Swedish and Russian but also in French, English, and German. The English romantics Wordsworth, Shelley, and Lord Byron, his "favourite poet", made a lasting impression.

In the poem "you say I am a riddle", which Nobel wrote during his first visit to Paris in 1851, you find an echo of this romantic idealism. The poem written in English, is largely autobiographical. It is dedicated to a "lovely girl", too early "wedded to her grave". It begins:

You say I am a riddle – it may be
for all of us are riddles unexplained.
Begun in pain, in deeper torture ended.
This breathing clay what business has it here?

During the busiest periods of his life, Nobel was forced to put his literary interests to one side, especially at the beginning of his career when experiments, financial problems, constant travelling, and a growing industrial empire absorbed most of his time. However, reading good literature was his main form of relaxation and he always took a book or two with him on his travels. One letter reveals that, even as late as at the age of 35, when some projects had gone awry, he considered abandoning business and his inventions and taking up writing for his livelihood.

Nobel settled in Paris, the capital of culture, at the age of 40. "Every mongrel here smells of civilisation", he noted with pleasure. Here he met Bertha von Suttner (later founder of the Austrian peace movement), a meeting which was to prove very important for Nobel, not because of the peace issue alone. When she first visited his home on Avenue Malakoff in 1876, Bertha was struck by his "well-stocked library, capable of satisfying the most divergent wishes". Her visit was brief, but they maintained a lifelong intellectual friendship, mainly through correspondence. His discussions with Bertha were to prove stimulating – on literary matters as well. She never failed to send him her works with a friendly dedication: "From your dear friend and comrade-in-arms", "a testimony of our friendship". Reading her work may well have influenced Nobel's own attitude to literature in "an ideal direction". This could apply not only to her description of society and her anti-war novel *Die Waffen nieder!* (Lay down Your Arms!, 1889) – her "admirable masterpiece", which he praised for its grand ideas and "charming style" – but also to works such as *Ein Manuscript!*(1885), where she reflected upon questions of a more private and aesthetic nature.

Juliette Adam-Lamber, who maintained a literary salon, wrote books, and published the magazine *La Nouvelle Revue,* was one of the few people whose company Nobel kept in Paris. He met Victor Hugo at her home and probably also younger writers like Pierre Loti, Paul Bourget, and Maupassant. Both Bertha von Suttner and Nobel had contacts with the literary circle linked to the more academic magazine *La Revue des Deux Mondes.* It is remarkable that despite his busy life he was able to keep up with current literature, and at that time he systematically added to his library contemporary literature not only in French but also in English, German and the Scandinavian languages. He also collected the classics in beautifully bound editions, Musset, Tegnér, Shakespeare, Scott, Goethe, Schiller, all writers that he quoted readily.

Among Norwegian writers he preferred Ibsen and Biornson (Nobel Prize 1903). His favourite Danish writer was the storyteller H.C. Andersen. Turgenev and Tolstoy were the Russian writers he valued. (There is no Dostoyevsky in his library.)

Among the French he most admired Victor Hugo, the pacifist, and the idealist, who felt such compassion for "les misérables", the social outcasts. Nobel was also invited from time to time to the aged laureate's home; they lived close to each other near the Bois-de-Boulogne.

Viktor Rydberg was the Swedish poet he held in greatest esteem. Rydberg's writing "denotes nobility of soul and beauty of form", he wrote. In another context Nobel described himself in the words: "I am a misanthrope and yet utterly benevolent, have more than one screw loose and am a super-idealist, a kind of ungifted Rydberg, I digest philosophy better than food."

Nobel's collection of books bears testimony to both the depth and breadth of his reading, even in fields such as philosophy, history, religion, and the history of science. He was familiar with Voltaire and Rousseau, the philosophers of the Enlightenment. He studied positivism and Comte with fervour, Comte's anti-religious and philosophical ideas about society corresponding to a large extent with his own. He also diligently inserted discreet penciled annotations in positivistically inspired works such as G.H. Lewe's *History of Philosophy,* Hippolyte Taine's *Les origines de la France contemporaine* and Henry Buckle's *History of Civilisation in England,* as well as in Gibbon's worldwide success *The History of the Decline and Fall of the Roman Empire,* Albert Schwegler's *Geschichte der Philosophie* and Karl von Rotteck's *Allgemeine Weltgeschichte,* with its rapturous idealism and love of liberty. Voltaire, Gibbon and Taine were almost certainly writers who appealed to him with their wit and distinctly clear style. In his old age, when he was in poor health, he was able to resume his writing. He had already started a socially critical novel before leaving St. Petersburg.

Nobel was in many respects a man of the pen: he was continuously writing letters, noting down all kinds of fanciful ideas and plans for inventions, philosophising over the origin of the cosmos and the evolution of man, discussing questions of faith and knowledge, war and peace. When he died, he left an extensive collection of letters: business correspondence, letters from his brothers and other close friends and relatives and copies of his own letters. At times he wrote twenty odd letters a day. Over the years he became a proficient correspondent, cleverly adapting language, and style to the recipient. Bertha von Suttner describes the beginning of their correspondence in her memoirs: "Mr Nobel and I exchanged several letters. He wrote soulful and intelligent letters, but in a melancholic tone. He seemed to be unhappy, misanthropic, highly cultured, and to own a deeply philosophical conception of the world. A Swede, whose other mother tongue was Russian, he wrote with the same accuracy and elegance in German, French and English."

In his private letters he liked to portray himself as a sickly old grumbler, ugly and unsociable. But they also bear testimony to a moving concern for his nearest and dearest, especially his mother and his brothers' children. In other letters his words can seem very caustic. When his brother Ludvig asked him in 1887 whether he did not wish to contribute to a biography of the Nobel family, his reply was: "For me writing biographies is impossible, unless they are brief and concise, and these are, I feel, the most eloquent. E.g. Alfred Nobel – pitiful halfling, should have been suffocated by a humane doctor, when he made his wailing entry into life. *Greatest merits:* keeping his nails clean and never being a burden to anyone. *Greatest defect:* lack of family, a happy disposition and a good stomach. *Greatest and only request:* not to be buried alive. *Greatest sin:* not worshipping Mammon. *Important events in his life:* none."

Nobel was obviously fascinated by language. In his youth his literary talents lay in poetry, later in life in the aphoristic and self-reflective. Concise expressions, pithy observations, often spiced with pungent humour and merciless self-criticism, were his distinguishing features.

Nobel's self-denial and misanthropy were, however, balanced by a solidly grounded belief in progress. Technological inventions and scientific conquests would lead humanity forwards, and he seems to have believed that good literature could play a dynamic role in an "ideal direction".

# ALFRED NOBEL THE POET

Loneliness, thirst for love, reflection on the meaning of life and the origin of the universe provide the fundamental themes of Alfred Nobel's autobiographical and melancholically inclined poetry, which consists of little more than a handful of works in finished manuscript form. The longest and most complete are written in English, in blank verse. The poems, including those written in Swedish, span a period from his youth to his later years. These essays in lyricism are the fruit of long and faithful acquaintance with the Romantic poets, particularly the English Romantics, Shelley, and Byron.

Nobel was an occasional poet: he mainly resorted to the pen in order to divert his thoughts when he felt lonely, was tired of business and plagued by intrigues. Then poetry was a source of energy and inspiration. In his personal and contemplative poetry, we encounter a little-known aspect of this otherwise famous inventor and endower of prizes. With one or two exceptions, these poems have remained concealed in Swedish archives for the best part of a century.

Why publish poems that Alfred Nobel himself never let publish, some, moreover, that were never completed? We also know that he guarded his integrity jealously, and that his shyness and reticence were legendary. However, there are some cogent reasons for making them public. One is that he himself took out some of his poems to send to outsiders for their assessment. Another is that although he was highly self-critical, he was not alien, as his letters show, to the idea of publishing one or two of his poems, if only for his own pleasure. Although the brilliance that surrounds the name of Nobel has intensified with the years and the Nobel prize awards, the man himself, the humanist, has become obscured, and indeed seems increasingly enigmatic. His poems offer no solution to the mystery, but they do bring us closer to this remarkable, many-faceted man who wrote his tragedy 'Nemesis' (1896), noted: "There is a philosophy of both feeling and thought" during  the last days of his life. Those who want to find out more about his emotional and intellectual life will find one opportunity here. In principle, lyric poetry is a genre of self-disclosure.

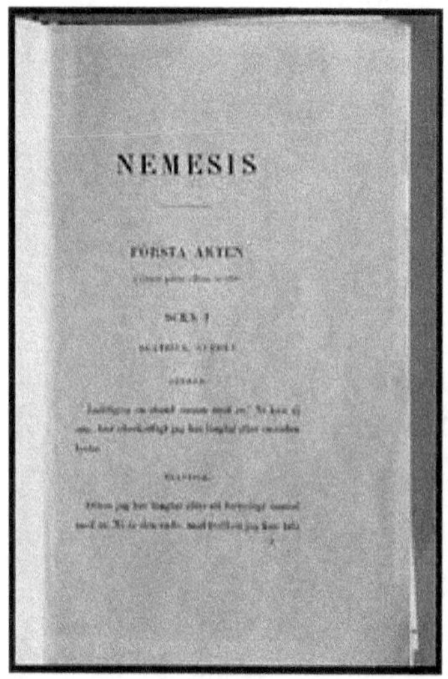

The play 'Nemesis' was written by Nobel during the last year of his life

It seems very natural to introduce the poet and cosmopolitan Nobel to an international audience. He wrote his most significant poems  in his native language as well as in English. It is also important to emphasize in this context that they were drafts. There would be little point in comparing him with his brilliant exemplars. It has already been pointed out that Shelley and Byron were among Nobel's favorite authors from his youth onwards. Words with poetic or archaic ring found in both the English Romantics can be recognized in Nobel's poetry

Nobel's letters reveal that he destroyed a great deal of youthful poetry. One of his earliest known essays in poetry ' A Riddle', which begins with the words "You say I am a riddle".* He was then 18 years old and the poem seems to have been written during his first stay in Paris, the outcome of a romantic disappointment. In October 1862, Alfred (then aged 29) sent an emotional letter in French and his poem *A Likeness* – a somewhat revised version of *A Riddle* – to "Mademoiselle" Olga de Fock who was living in the manor house at Maanselkä in Karelia. He included G.H. Lewes' novel *Ranthorpe*. Alfred is upset about a rumor claiming that he has time to write poetry.

According to Bertha von Suttner Nobel's tragedy is well written. At the same time, she remembers his unpublished essays in poetry that she had been shown two decades earlier. She mentioned "His studies, his books and experiments – they occupied the whole of his life. He was also a writer and a poet, but he never published any of his poetic works. He gave me the manuscript of a hundred-page poem, written in English – I thought it was simply magnificent."

In 1895 Nobel drew up a list of his scientific and literary projects. In a category headed "Literature and Poetry" he records 14 titles, including drafts for novels, dramas and lyric poetry, this latter genre predominating. The list also reveals, which is interesting, that even late in life he had several literary projects in mind.

Everything suggests that the young Alfred, at the most malleable stage of his life, encountered in his reading the great Romantic poets, those writing in English. He was to foster this deep interest for his entire lifetime.

*please find full poem "you say I am a riddle" in annexure II

# ALFRED NOBEL – LIFE AND PHILOSOPHY

We know that he had literary interests and ambitions. He was an avid reader of fiction and wrote his own dramatic works and poems. In addition, he was attracted to philosophical issues. He read certain philosophical works with such interest that he underlined important passages. Among the papers that he left behind is a black notebook on philosophy that his biographers have not taken an interest in it. Although not constituting profound original thoughts, these penciled notes reflect his serious interest in philosophical questions. Nobel went through philosophy from antiquity to modern times, pointing out what he perceived to be vital issues. He made his own comments, where a morose way showed his detachment from the subject. He commented on Plato, Aristotle, and Democritus, but also on Newton and Voltaire as well as contemporary biologists such as Darwin and Haeckel.

Nobel wrote that all science is built on observations of similarities and differences. He continued:

"A chemical analysis is of course nothing other than this, and even mathematics has no other foundation. History is a picture of past similarities and differences; geography shows the differences in the earth's surface; geology, similarities, and differences in the earth's formation, from which we deduce the course of its transformations. Astronomy is the study of similarities and differences between celestial bodies; physics, a study of similarities and differences that arise from the attraction and motive functions of matter. The only exception to this rule is religious doctrine, but even this rests on the similar gullibility of most people. Even metaphysics – if it is not too insane – must find support for its hypotheses in analogy. One can state, without exaggeration, that the observation of and the search for similarities and differences are the basis of all human knowledge."

Alfred Nobel also viewed himself with detachment, or shall we say, philosophical scepticism. He often described himself as a loner, hermit, melancholic or misanthrope. He once wrote: "I am a misanthrope and yet utterly benevolent, have more than one screw loose yet am a super-idealist who digests philosophy more efficiently than food." Even from this description, this misanthrope was also a philanthropist, or what Nobel called a super-idealist. It was the idealist in him that drove Nobel to bequeath his fortune to those who had benefited humanity through science, literature, and efforts to promote peace.

Nobel's will was hardly longer than one ordinary page. After listing bequests to relatives and other people close to him, Nobel declared that his entire remaining estate should be used to endow "prizes to those who, during the preceding year, shall have conferred the greatest benefit to mankind." His will attracted attention throughout the world. It was unusual at that time to donate large sums of money for scientific and charitable purposes. Many people also criticized the international character of the prizes, saying they should be restricted to Swedes. This would not have suited the cosmopolitan Alfred Nobel. Some of his relatives contested the will. Complicated legal and administrative matters also had to be sorted out. All this took time, but eventually it was all settled.

In 1901, the first Nobel Prizes were awarded. The donor himself could hardly have dreamed of the impact that his benevolence would have in the future.

The commemorative medal that has been struck for this occasion — designed by the artist Rune Karlzon — is intended to remind us of some of Alfred Nobel's various activities. The back of the medal shows a tunnel blasted by dynamite and a detonator or blasting cap. On the front of the medal is a portrait of Nobel, with the Latin inscription *Creavit et promovit,* which can be translated "He created and promoted." This sums up, in the briefest possible way, the remarkable accomplishments of Alfred Nobel.

# ALFRED NOBLE'S THOUGHTS ABOUT WAR AND PEACE

When Alfred Nobel's will was made known after his death in San Remo on 10 December 1896, and when it was disclosed that he had established a special peace prize, this immediately created a great international sensation. The name Nobel related to explosives and with inventions useful to the art of making war, but certainly not with questions related to peace.

Alfred Nobel's will prescribed that the Peace Prize was to be awarded by a committee of five persons chosen by the Norwegian Parliament (Storting) and should go to the person who accomplished "the most or the best work for fraternity among nations, for the abolition or reduction of standing armies and for the promotion of peace congresses."

In the literature on Alfred Nobel, there exist different interpretations of his ideas and involvement in the peace question. In some works, it is claimed that the interest in peace accompanied Alfred Nobel since his youth, in others that he did not come to reflect over questions of mankind's fate until quite late.

Alfred Nobel had a clear view of what was happening in international politics during the second half of the 19th century. His own activity as an industrialist was to the utmost degree, international and it was vitally necessary for him to follow this development carefully. Important portions of his inventions and business activity related to conditions which affected war and peace.

Alfred Nobel's direct involvement in the war materiel sector did not come about until during the later stages of his life. It was also at this time that his interest in the question of peace came into practical expression. His thoughts on war and peace were set out in many years of correspondence with the Austrian peace partisan and authoress of the famous anti-war novel "Lay down Your Arms", Bertha von Suttner.

According to the Austrian countess Bertha von Suttner, Alfred Nobel, as early as their first meeting in Paris in 1876, had expressed his wish to produce material or a machine which would have such a devastating effect that war from then on, would be impossible. The point about deterrence later appeared among Nobel's ideas. In 1891, he commented on his dynamite factories by saying to the countess: "Perhaps my factories will put an end to war sooner than your congresses: on the day that two army corps can mutually annihilate each other in a second, all civilised nations will surely recoil with horror and disband their troops." Nobel did not live long enough to experience the First World War and to see how wrong his conception was.

Nobel's contact with Bertha von Suttner obviously had its impact on his thinking, at least to a certain point. The countess was a driving force in the international peace movement which developed in Europe during the latter part of the 19th century, and she tried energetically to get Nobel to engage himself in this activity, but with limited success. To be sure, he became a member of the Austrian Peace Association and supported it with money. But, as he frankly wrote to her, it was not money, which was most needed, but a realistic program. In his own words: "Good wishes alone will not ensure peace." Despite his pronounced scepticism towards peace associations and peace congresses, Alfred Nobel continued to observe the peace work in Europe. He even employed a former Turkish diplomat, Aristarchi Bey, with the main task to keep Nobel *au courant* with the activities of the peace movements, including the study of new procedures of conflict resolution, for instance establishing some sort of international court. Some of these ideas have later recurred in international politics, then under the comprehensive designation of "collective security".

Even if Alfred Nobel for a long time maintained a certain cool distance to the international peace association's methods, his interest in a donation to the promotion of world peace was influenced by Bertha von Suttner.

Evidently, Alfred Nobel did not consider his involvement in the war materials industry and in the work for world peace as incompatible elements. Rather he gave expression to the prevalent 19th century understanding which maintained, that the scientist was not responsible for how his findings were used. Each scholarly discovery is neutral but can be used both for good and bad objectives. And when it was applied to weapons, Nobel held firm to his old opinion that this had a deterrent effect above all.

The main source relating to Alfred Nobel's thoughts on war and peace is his own archive, kept in the Swedish National Archives, Stockholm, and catalogued in 1972 by Robert Svedlund. Here, one can study Nobel's extensive correspondence, which includes originals of the letters he received and copies of his own letters – sometimes of a technical quality that renders them partly illegible. Of use for the present paper, have primarily been the letters sent from Bertha von Suttner to Alfred Nobel: seventy or so letters, as well as cards, clippings, and brochures from the period 1891-1896. Of interest also are about sixty letters, reports and press clippings from the former Turkish diplomat, Gregoris Aristarchi Bey, from 1891 to 1892, the time when he was employed by Nobel to keep a special watch over the development of the peace question.

Considering the importance of the correspondence between Nobel and Bertha von Suttner, it can be noted that in her private archive, kept in the League of Nation's library archive in Geneva, there exist more original letters in Nobel's hand than can be found in his book of copies. Several of the letters are published in her book "Memoiren" (1909), which is also based on the diaries kept in the Geneva archives. An interesting portrait of Alfred Nobel can also be found in Bertha von Suttner's "Stimmen und Gestalten" (1907).

Other works, on the other hand, have underlined Bertha von Suttner's influence. This is particularly true of Irwin Abrams article in the *Journal of Central European Affairs* (1962) entitled "Bertha von Suttner and the Nobel Peace Prize." Here, Abrams made use of von Suttner's archive in Geneva.

# APHORISMS BY ALFRED NOBEL

Literature occupied a central role in the life of Alfred Nobel. He regarded various literary forms of expression as opportunities to achieve a greater understanding of our own thoughts, lives and relationships with other people and our surroundings. Alfred Nobel had an extensive library, which included important European literary works. Inspired by Shelley and Byron, he wrote poems in English as a young man. Toward the end of his life, he wrote the tragedy *Nemesis*. His best literary form of expression was probably the aphorism, where he often expressed himself drastically.

"A heart can no more be forced to love than a stomach can be forced to digest food by persuasion."

"Second to agriculture, humbug is the biggest industry of our age."

"Contentment is the only real wealth."

"We build upon the sand, and the older we become, the more unstable this foundation becomes."

"The truthful man is usually a liar."

"Justice is to be found only in the imagination."

"It is not sufficient to be worthy of respect in order to be respected."

"Worry is the stomach's worst poison."

"The best excuse for the fallen ones is that Madame Justice herself is one of them."

"Self-respect without the respect of others is like a jewel which will not stand the daylight."

"Hope is nature's veil for hiding truth's nakedness."

"Lying is the greatest of all sins."

"Home is where I work, and I work everywhere."

# ALFRED NOBEL'S WILL: THE ESTABLISHMENT OF THE NOBEL PRIZE

"All of my remaining realisable assets are to be disbursed as follows: the capital, converted to safe securities by my executors, is to constitute a fund, the interest on which is to be distributed annually as prizes to those who, during the preceding year, have conferred the greatest benefit to humankind. The interest is to be divided into five equal parts and distributed as follows: one part to the person who made the most important discovery or invention in the field of physics; one part to the person who made the most important chemical discovery or improvement; one part to the person who made the most important discovery within the domain of physiology or medicine; one part to the person who, in the field of literature, produced the most outstanding work in an idealistic direction; and one part to the person who has done the most or best to advance fellowship among nations, the abolition or reduction of standing armies, and the establishment and promotion of peace congresses. The prizes for physics and chemistry are to be awarded by the Swedish Academy of Sciences; that for physiological or medical achievements by the Karolinska Institute in Stockholm; that for literature by the Academy in Stockholm; and that for champions of peace by a committee of five persons to be selected by the Norwegian Storting. It is my express wish that when awarding the prizes, no consideration be given to nationality, but that the prize be awarded to the worthiest person, whether or not they are Scandinavian."

# NOBLE PRIZE FACTS

On 27 November 1895, Alfred Nobel signed his last will and testament, giving the largest share of his fortune to a series of prizes in Physics, Chemistry, Physiology or Medicine, Literature and Peace – the Nobel Prizes. In 1968, Sveriges Riksbank (Sweden's central bank) established The Sveriges Riksbank Prize in Economic Sciences in Memory of Alfred Nobel. Learn more about the Nobel Laureates here.

## 597 Nobel Prizes

Between 1901 and 2019, the Nobel Prizes and the Prize in Economic Sciences were awarded 597 times.

| Nobel Prize | Number of Prizes | Number of Laureates | Awarded to one Laureate | Shared by two Laureates | Shared by three Laureates |
|---|---|---|---|---|---|
| **Physics** | 113 | 213 | 47 | 32 | 34 |
| **Chemistry** | 111 | 184 | 63 | 23 | 25 |
| **Medicine** | 110 | 219 | 39 | 33 | 38 |
| **Literature** | 112 | 116 | 108 | 4 | – |
| **Peace** | 100 | 107+27 | 68 | 30 | 2 |
| **Economic Sciences** | 51 | 84 | 25 | 19 | 7 |
| *Total:* | **597** | **950** | **350** | **141** | **106** |

In the statutes of the Nobel Foundation it says: "A prize amount may be equally divided between two works, each of which is considered to merit a prize. If a work that is being rewarded has been produced by two or three persons, the prize shall be awarded to them jointly. In no case may a prize amount be divided between more than three persons.

923 Laureates and 27 organizations have been awarded the Nobel Prize between 1901 and 2019. Of them, 84 are Laureates in Economic Sciences. A small number of individuals and organizations have been honored more than once, which means that 919 individuals and 24 unique organizations have received the Nobel Prize in total.

## Years without Nobel Prizes

The Nobel Prize Medal. Photo: Alexander Mahmoud 2018

Since the start, in 1901, there are some years when the Nobel Prizes have not been awarded. The total number of times are 49. Most of them during World War I (1914-1918) and II (1939-1945) In the statutes of the Nobel Foundation it says: "If none of the works under consideration is found to be of the importance indicated in the first paragraph, the prize money shall be reserved until the following year. If, even then, the prize cannot be awarded, the amount shall be added to the Foundation's restricted funds.".

**Physics:** 1916, 1931, 1934, 1940, 1941, 1942

**Chemistry:** 1916, 1917, 1919, 1924, 1933, 1940, 1941, 1942

**Medicine:** 1915, 1916, 1917, 1918, 1921, 1925, 1940, 1941, 1942

**Literature:**  1914, 1918, 1935, 1940, 1941, 1942, 1943

**Peace:** 1914, 1915, 1916, 1918, 1923, 1924, 1928, 1932, 1939, 1940, 1941, 1942, 1943, 1948, 1955, 1956, 1966, 1967, 1972

**Economic Sciences:** –

## The youngest Nobel Laureates

| Age | Name | Category/Year | Date of birth |
|---|---|---|---|
| 17 | Malala Yousafzai | Peace 2014 | 12 July 1997 |
| 25 | Lawrence Bragg | Physics 1915 | 31 March 1890 |
| 25 | Nadia Murad | Peace 2018 | 1993 |
| 31 | Werner Heisenberg | Physics 1932 | 5 December 1901 |
| 31 | Tsung-Dao Lee | Physics 1957 | 24 November 1926 |
| 31 | Carl D. Anderson | Physics 1936 | 3 September 1905 |
| 31 | Paul A. M. Dirac | Physics 1933 | 8 August 1902 |
| 32 | Frederick G. Banting | Medicine 1923 | 14 November 1891 |
| 32 | Tawakkol Karman | Peace 2011 | 7 February 1979 |
| 32 | Rudolf Mossbauer | Physics 1961 | 31 January 1929 |
| 32 | Mairead Corrigan | Peace 1976 | 27 January 1944 |
| 33 | Joshua Lederberg | Medicine 1958 | 23 May 1925 |
| 33 | Betty Williams | Peace 1976 | 22 May 1943 |
| 33 | Rigoberta Menchu Tum | Peace 1992 | 9 January 1959 |

| Category | Name | Year of Award | Age of Nobel Laureate |
|---|---|---|---|
| Physics | William Lawrence Bragg | 1915 | 25 |
| Chemistry | Frederic Joliot | 1935 | 35 |
| Physiology or Medicine | Frederick Banting | 1923 | 32 |
| Literature | Rudyard Kipling | 1907 | 41 |
| Peace | Malala Yousafzai | 2014 | 17 |
| Economic Sciences | Esther Duflo | 2019 | 46 |

## The oldest Nobel Laureates

| Age | Name | Category/Year | Date of birth |
|---|---|---|---|
| 97 | John B. Goodenough | Chemistry 2019 | 1922 |
| 96 | Authur Ashkin | Physics 2018 | 2 September 1922 |
| 90 | Leonid Hurwicz | Economic Sciences 2007 | 21 August 1917 |
| 89 | Lloyd Shapley | Economic Sciences 2012 | 2 June 1923 |
| 88 | Raymond Davis Jr. | Physics 2002 | 14 October 1914 |
| 88 | Doris Lessing | Literature 2007 | 22 October 1919 |
| 87 | Yoichiro Nambu | Physics 2008 | 18 January 1921 |
| 87 | Vitaly L. Ginzburg | Physics 2003 | 4 October 1916 |
| 87 | Peyton Rous | Medicine 1966 | 5 October 1879 |
| 87 | Joseph Rotblat | Peace 1995 | 4 November 1908 |
| 87 | Karl von Frisch | Medicine 1973 | 20 November 1886 |

| 85 | Ferdinand Buisson | Peace 1927 | 20 December 1841 |
|----|-------------------|------------|------------------|
| 85 | John B. Fenn | Chemistry 2002 | 15 June 1917 |
| 85 | Theodor Mommsen | Literature 1902 | 30 November 1817 |
| 85 | Williard S. Boyle | Physics 2009 | 19 August 1929 |

| Category | Name | Year of Award | Age of Nobel Laureate |
|----------|------|---------------|-----------------------|
| Physics | Arthur Ashkin | 2018 | 96 |
| Chemistry | John B. Goodenough | 2019 | 97 |
| Physiology or Medicine | Peyton Rous | 1966 | 87 |
| Literature | Doris Lessing | 2007 | 88 |
| Peace | Joseph Rotblat | 1995 | 87 |
| Economic Sciences | Leonid Hurwicz | 2007 | 90 |

## 54 Nobel Prizes to women

Between 1901 and 2019, total 54 women's have received the Nobel Prize and Prize in Economic Sciences award.

## Two Nobel Laureates declined the prize

Jean-Paul Sartre, awarded the 1964 Nobel Prize in Literature, declined the prize because he had consistently declined all official honors.

Le Duc Tho awarded the 1973 Nobel Peace Prize jointly with US Secretary of State Henry Kissinger. They were awarded the Prize for negotiating the Vietnam peace accord. Le Doc Tho said that he was not in a position to accept the Nobel Peace Prize, citing the situation in Vietnam as his reason.

## Forced to decline the Nobel Prize

Four Nobel Laureates have been forced by authorities to decline the Nobel Prize. Adolf Hitler forbade three German Nobel Laureates, **Richard Kuhn, Adolf Butenandt,** and **Gerhard Domagk,** from accepting the Nobel Prize. All of them could later receive the Nobel Prize Diploma and Medal, but not the prize amount.

**Boris Pasternak** the 1958 Nobel Laureate in Literature initially accepted the Nobel Prize but was later coerced by the authorities of the Soviet Union, his native country, to decline the Nobel Prize.

## Nobel Laureates under arrest at the time of the award

Three Nobel Laureates were under arrest at the time of the award of the Nobel Prize, all of them Nobel Peace Prize Laureates:

German pacifist and journalist **Carl von Ossietzky**
Burmese politician **Anung San Suu Kyi**
Chinese human rights activist **Liu Xiaobo**

## Multiple Nobel Laureates

The work of the International Committee of the Red Cross (ICRC) has been honored by a Nobel Peace Prize three times.

Linus Pauling is the only person to have been awarded two unshared Nobel Prizes – the 1954 Nobel Prize in Chemistry and the 1962 Nobel Peace Prize.

| J. Bardeen | M. Curie | L. Pauling |
|---|---|---|
| Physics 1956<br>Physics 1972 | Physics 1903<br>Chemistry 1911 | Chemistry 1954<br>Peace 1962 |
| F. Sanger | ICRC | UNHCR |
| Chemistry 1958<br>Chemistry 1980 | Peace 1917<br>Peace 1944<br>Peace 1963 | Peace 1954<br>Peace 1981 |

## "Family Nobel Laureates"

The Curies were a very successful 'Nobel Prize family'. Marie Curie herself was awarded two Nobel Prizes.

| Married couples (at the time of the award) | | |
|---|---|---|
| Marie Curie<br>Pierre Curie | Irene Joliot-Curie<br>Frederic Joliot | Gerty Cori<br>Carl Cori |
| May-Britt Moser<br>Edvard I. Moser | Alva Myrdal<br>Gunnar Myrdal | Esther Duflo<br>Abhijit Banerjee |

| **Mother & daughter** | | |
| --- | --- | --- |
| Marie Curie<br>Irene Joliot-Curie | | |
| **Father & daughter** | | |
| Pierre Curie<br>Irene Joliot-Curie | | |
| **Father & son** | | |
| William Bragg<br>Lawrence Bragg | Niels Bohr<br>Aage N. Bohr | Hans von Euler-Chelpin<br>Ulf von Euler |
| Arthur Kornberg<br>Roger D. Kornberg | Manne Siegbahn<br>Kai M. Siegbahn | J. J. Thomson<br>George Paget Thomson |
| **Brothers** | | |
| Jan Tinbergen<br>Nikolaas Tinbergen | | |

## The Nobel Prize insignias

At the Nobel Prize Award Ceremonies on 10 December the Nobel Laureates receive three things: a Nobel diploma, a Nobel Medal and a document confirming the Nobel Prize amount. Each Nobel diploma is a unique work of art, created by foremost Swedish and Norwegian artists and calligraphers. The Nobel Medals are handmade with careful precision and in 18 carat recycled gold.

The Nobel Medals in Physics, Chemistry, Physiology or Medicine and Literature are identical on the face: it shows the image of Alfred Nobel and the years of his birth and death (1833-1896). Nobel's portrait also appears on the Nobel Peace Prize Medal and the Medal for the Prize in Economic Sciences, but with a slightly different design. The image on the reverse varies according to the institution awarding the prize.

## The Nobel Prize amount

Alfred Nobel left most of his estate, more than SEK 31 million (today approximately SEK 1,702 million) to be converted into a fund and invested in "safe securities." The income from the investments was to be "distributed annually in the form of prizes to those who during the preceding year have conferred the greatest benefit to mankind."

The Nobel Prize amount for 2019 is set at Swedish kronor (SEK) 9.0 million per full Nobel Prize.

# PHYSICS

Alfred Nobel has mentioned Physics the first prize area in his will. At the end of the nineteenth century, many people considered physics as the foremost of the sciences, and perhaps Nobel saw it this way as well. His own research was also closely tied to physics. The Nobel Prize in Physics is awarded by The Royal Swedish Academy of Science, Stockholm, Sweden.

## About the Prize:

On 27 November 1895, Alfred Nobel signed his last will and testament, giving the largest share of his fortune to a series of prizes, the Nobel Prizes. As described in Nobel's will, one part was dedicated to "the person who shall have made the most important discovery or invention within the field of physics".

**Learn more about the Nobel Prize in Physics from 1901 to 2019.**

| | |
|---|---|
| Nobel Prizes in Physics have been awarded since 1901 | 113 |
| Nobel Prizes in Physics not awarded on six occasions | in 1916, 1931, 1934, 1940, 1941, and 1942. |
| Physics Prizes have been given to one Laureate only. | 47 |
| Physics Prizes have been shared by two Laureates. | 32 |
| Physics Prizes have been shared between three Laureates. | 34 |
| Total number of laureates in Physics (1901-2019.) | 213* Laureates |

| | |
|---|---|
| The youngest Nobel Laureate in Physics | Lawrence Bragg (25 when awarded) |
| The oldest Nobel Laureate in Physics | Arthur Ashkin (96 when awarded) |
| Female Nobel laureates in Physics | 1903 –Marie Curie<br>1963 – Maria Goeppert Mayer<br>2018 – Donna Strickland |
| Multiple Nobel laureates in Physics | John Brdeen in physics twice, year 1956 and 1972<br><br>Marie Currie- in Physics 1903 and in Chemistry 1911. |
| Couple Nobel laureates in Physics | Marie Curie and Pierre Curie (1903) |
| Father & son Nobel laureates in Physics | William Bragg and Lawrence Bragg 1915<br><br>Niels Bohr 1922 and Aage N. Bohr 1975<br><br>Manne Siegbahn 1924 and Kai M. Siegbahn 1981<br><br>J. J. Thomson 1906 and George Paget Thomson 1937 |

*As John Bardeen has been awarded twice there are **212** individuals who have been awarded the Nobel Prize in Physics since 1901.

**Nomination and selection procedure to the Nobel prize in physics:**

Nomination to the Nobel prize in physics and chemistry is same and by invitation only. The names of the nominees and other information about the nominations cannot be revealed until 50 years later.

The Nobel Committee for Physics and chemistry sends confidential forms to persons who are competent and qualified to nominate.

How are the Nobel Laureates selected?

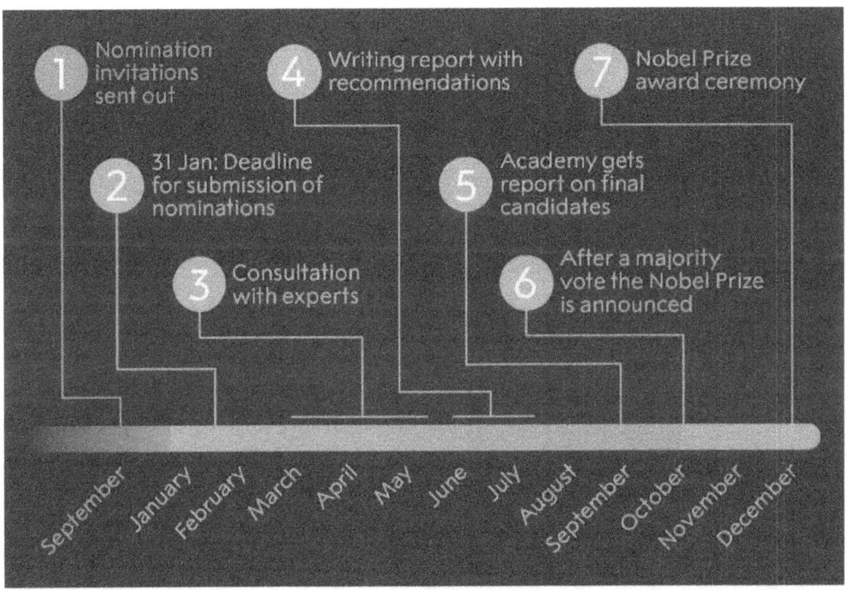


The nomination process for Nobel Laureates in physics and chemistry  Ill.N. Elmehed

## The process involved in selecting the Nobel Laureate

**September** – *Nomination forms are sent out.*

(The Nobel Committee sends out confidential forms to around 3,000 people – selected professors at universities around the world, Nobel Laureates in Physics and members of the Royal Swedish Academy of Sciences, among others.)

**February** – *Deadline for submission.*

(The completed nomination forms must reach the Nobel Committee no later than 31 January of the following year. The Committee screens the nominations and selects the preliminary candidates. About 250–350 names are nominated as several nominators often submit the same name.)

**March-May** – *Consultation with experts.*

(The Nobel Committee sends the names of the preliminary candidates to specially appointed experts for their assessment of the candidates' work.)

**June-August** – *Writing of the report.*

(The Nobel Committee puts together the report with recommendations to be submitted to the Academy. The report is signed by all members of the Committee.)

**September** – *Committee submits recommendations.*

(The Nobel Committee submits its report with recommendations on the final candidates to the members of the Academy. The report is discussed at two meetings of the Physics Class of the Academy.)

## October – *Nobel Laureates are chosen.*

(In early October, the Academy selects the Nobel Laureates in Physics through a majority vote. The decision is final and without appeal. The names of the Nobel Laureates are then announced.)

## December – *Nobel Laureates receive their prize.*

(The Nobel Prize Award Ceremony takes place on 10 December in Stockholm, where the Nobel Laureates receive their Nobel Prize, which consists of a Nobel Medal and Diploma, and a document confirming the prize amount.)

### Are the nominations made public?

The statutes of the Nobel Foundation restrict disclosure of information about the nominations, whether publicly or privately, for 50 years. The restriction concerns the nominees and nominators, as well as investigations and opinions related to the award of a prize.

# CHEMISTRY

Alfred Nobel has mentioned chemistry the second prize area in his will, however chemistry was the most important science for Alfred Nobel's own work, the development of his inventions as well as the industrial processes he employed were based upon chemical knowledge. The Nobel Prize in Chemistry is awarded by The Royal Swedish Academy of Science, Stockholm, Sweden.

## About the Prize:

On 27 November 1895, Alfred Nobel signed his last will and testament, giving the largest share of his fortune to a series of prizes, the Nobel Prizes. As described in Nobel's will one part was dedicated to "the person who shall have made the most important chemical discovery or improvement".

**Learn more about the Nobel Prize in Chemistry from 1901 to 2019.**

| | |
|---|---|
| Nobel Prizes in Chemistry have been awarded since 1901 | 111 |
| Nobel Prizes in Chemistry not awarded on eight occasions | in 1916, 1917, 1919, 1924, 1933, 1940, 1941 and 1942. |
| Chemistry Prizes have been given to one Laureate only. | 63 |
| Chemistry Prizes have been shared by two Laureates. | 23 |
| Chemistry Prizes have been shared between three Laureates. | 25 |

| | |
|---|---|
| Total number of laureates in Chemistry (1901-2019.) | 184 Laureates* |
| The youngest Nobel Laureate in Chemistry | Frederic Joliot (35 when awarded) 1935 together with his wife, Irene Joliot-Curie. |
| The oldest Nobel Laureate in Chemistry | John B. Goodenough (97 when awarded) oldest Laureate to be awarded in all Prize categories. |
| Female Nobel laureates in Chemistry | 1911 – Marie Curie<br>1935 – Irene Joliot-Curie<br>1964 – Dorothy Crowfoot Hodgkin<br>2009 – Ada Yonath<br>2018 – Frances H. Arnold |
| Multiple Nobel laureates in Chemistry | Marie Curie<br>Physics 1903<br>Chemistry 1911<br><br>Linus Pauling<br>chemistry 1954<br>Peace 1962<br><br>Frederick Sanger<br>Chemistry 1958<br>Chemistry1980 |
| Couple Nobel laureates in Chemistry | Irene Joliot-Curie and Frederic Joliot 1935 |
| Father & son Nobel laureates in Chemistry | Hans von Euler-Chelpin in chemistry 1929 and Ulf von Euler in medicine 1970 |

|  | Arthur Kornberg in Medicine 1959 and Roger D. Kornberg in Chemistry 2006 |
| --- | --- |

*As Frederick Sanger has been awarded twice, there are **183** individuals who have received the Nobel Prize in Chemistry since 1901.

## Nomination and selection procedure to the Nobel prize in chemistry:

Nomination to the Nobel prize in **chemistry** is by invitation only. The names of the nominees and other information about the nominations cannot be revealed until 50 years later.

The Nobel Committee for chemistry sends confidential forms to persons who are competent and qualified to nominate.

How are the Nobel Laureates selected?

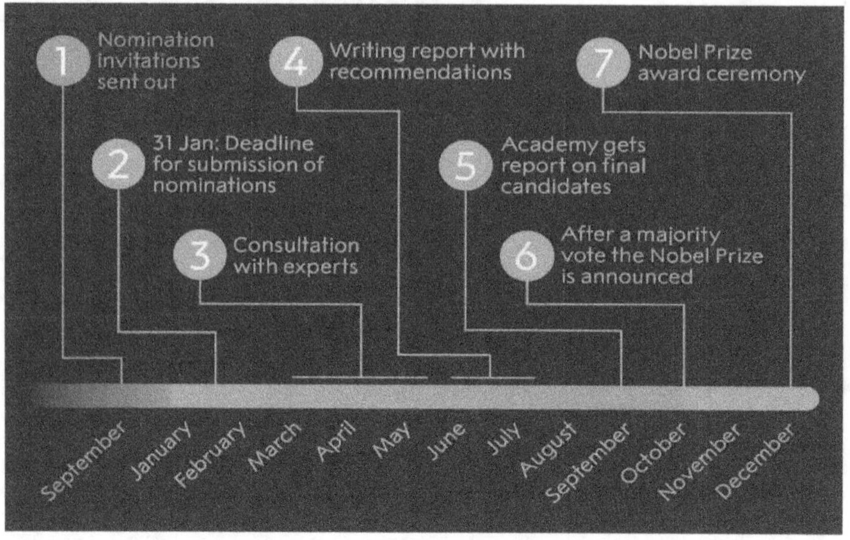


The nomination process for Nobel Laureates in chemistry  Ill.N. Elmehed

# The process involved in selecting the Nobel Laureate

**September** – *Nomination forms are sent out.*

(The Nobel Committee sends out confidential forms to around 3,000 people – selected professors at universities around the world, Nobel Laureates in Chemistry, and members of the Royal Swedish Academy of Sciences, among others.)

**February** – *Deadline for submission.*

(The completed nomination forms must reach the Nobel Committee no later than 31 January of the following year. The Committee screens the nominations and selects the preliminary candidates. About 250–350 names are nominated as several nominators often submit the same name.)

**March-May** – *Consultation with experts.*

(The Nobel Committee sends the names of the preliminary candidates to specially appointed experts for their assessment of the candidates' work.)

**June-August** – *Writing of the report.*

(The Nobel Committee puts together the report with recommendations to be submitted to the Academy. The report is signed by all members of the Committee.)

**September** – *Committee submits recommendations.*

(The Nobel Committee submits its report with recommendations on the final candidates to the members of the Academy. The report is discussed at two meetings of the Physics Class of the Academy.)

**October** – *Nobel Laureates are chosen.*

(In early October, the Academy selects the Nobel Laureates in chemistry through a majority vote. The decision is final and without appeal. The names of the Nobel Laureates are then announced.)

**December** – *Nobel Laureates receive their prize.*

(The Nobel Prize Award Ceremony takes place on 10 December in Stockholm, where the Nobel Laureates receive their Nobel Prize, which consists of a Nobel Medal and Diploma, and a document confirming the prize amount.)

**Are the nominations made public?**
The statutes of the Nobel Foundation restrict disclosure of information about the nominations, whether publicly or privately, for 50 years. The restriction concerns the nominees and nominators, as well as investigations and opinions related to the award of a prize.

# MEDICINE

Alfred Nobel had an active interest in medical research. Through Karolinska Institutet (institute), he encountered Swedish physiologist Jons Johansson around 1890. Johansson worked in Nobel's laboratory in Sevran, France during a brief period the same year. Physiology or medicine was the third prize area Nobel mentioned in his will.

The Nobel Prize in Physiology or Medicine is awarded by the Nobel Assembly at Karolinska Institutet, Stockholm, Sweden.

## About the Prize:

On 27 November 1895, Alfred Nobel signed his last will and testament, giving the largest share of his fortune to a series of prizes, the Nobel Prizes. As described in Nobel's will, one part was dedicated to "the person who shall have made the most important discovery within the domain of physiology or medicine".

**Learn more about the Nobel Prize in Physiology or Medicine from 1901 to 2019**

| | |
|---|---|
| Nobel Prizes in Medicine have been awarded since 1901 | 110 |
| Nobel Prizes in Medicine not awarded on nine occasions | in 1915, 1916, 1917, 1918, 1921, 1925, 1940, 1941 and 1942. |
| Medicine Prizes have been given to one Laureate only. | 39 |
| Medicine Prizes have been shared by two Laureates. | 33 |

| | |
|---|---|
| Medicine Prizes have been shared between three Laureates. | 38 |
| Total number of laureates in Medicine (1901-2019.) | 219 Laureates |
| The youngest Nobel Laureate in Medicine | Frederick G. Banting (32 when awarded) |
| The oldest Nobel Laureate in Medicine | Peyton Rous (87 when awarded), |
| Female Nobel laureates in Medicine | 1947 –Gerty Cori<br>1977 –Rosalyn Yalow<br>1983 – Barbara McClintock*<br>1986 – Rita Levi-Montalcini<br>1988 – Gertrude B. Elion<br>1995 –Christiane Nusslein-Volhard   2004 –Linda B. Buck            2008 – Francoise Barre-Sinoussi<br>2009 –Elizabeth H. Blackburn and Carol  W. Greider<br>2014 – May-Britt Moser<br>2015 –Tu Youyou |
| Multiple Nobel laureates in Medicine | No one has been awarded the Nobel Prize in Physiology or Medicine more than once Yet |
| Couple Nobel laureates in Medicine | Gerty Cori and Carl Cori (1947)<br><br>May-Britt Moser and Edvard I. Moser (2014) |
| Father & son Nobel laureates in Medicine | Hans von Euler-Chelpin (Chemistry Prize) and Ulf von Euler (Medicine Prize) |

|  | Arthur Kornberg (Medicine Prize) and Roger D. Kornberg (Chemistry Prize) |
|---|---|
| Brothers Nobel laureates in Medicine | Jan Tinbergen (Economics Prize) and Nikolaas Tinbergen (Medicine Prize) |

*Of these 12, Barabara McClintock is the only one who has received an unshared Nobel Prize.

## Nomination and selection procedure to the Nobel prize in physiology or medicine

Nomination to the Nobel prize in physiology or medicine is by invitation only. The names of the nominees and other information about the nominations and selection process cannot be revealed until 50 years later.

The Nobel Committee sends confidential invitation letters to persons who are competent and qualified to nominate candidates for the Nobel Prize in Physiology or Medicine.

### Selection of Nobel Laureates

The Nobel Assembly at Karolinska Institutet is responsible for the selection of the Nobel Laureates in Physiology or Medicine from among the candidates recommended by the Nobel Committee for Physiology or Medicine. The Nobel Assembly has 50 members. The Nobel Committee is the working body that reviews the nominations and selects the candidates. It consists of five members and the Secretary of the Nobel Committee and Nobel Assembly.

## Who is eligible for the Nobel Prize in Physiology or Medicine?

Candidates eligible for the Medicine Prize are those nominated by nominators who have received an invitation from the Nobel Committee to submit names for consideration. No one can nominate herself or himself.

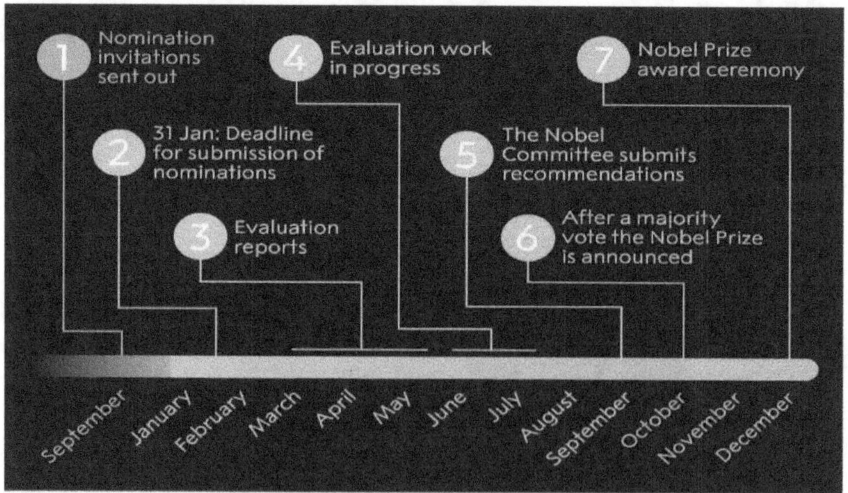


The nomination process for Nobel Laureates in Physiology or Medicine Ill. N. Elmehed

## The selecting process of the Nobel laureates in physiology or medicine prize.

**September** – *Invitation to nominate sent out.*

(Over 3000 personal confidential invitations sent out to qualified nominators.)

**February** – *Deadline for submission.*

(The completed forms must reach the Nobel Committee no later than 31 January of the following year.)

**March-May** – *Evaluation reports.*

(The Nobel Committee invites international reputable experts to prepare evaluation reports.)

**June-August** – *Evaluation work in progress.*

(Reports submitted by middle of August.)

**September** – *The Nobel Committee submits recommendations.*
(The Nobel Committee submits recommendations on presumable candidates for discussion in the Nobel Assembly.)

**October** – *The Nobel Prize in Physiology or Medicine is announced.*

(The Nobel Assembly chooses the Nobel Laureates in Physiology or Medicine through a majority vote on the first Monday in October. The decision is final and without appeal. The Nobel Laureates are informed immediately afterwards, and the decision is then announced at the press conference.)

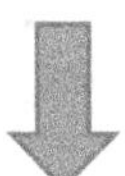

**December** – *The Nobel Prize Award Ceremony.*

(The Nobel Prize Award Ceremony takes place on the 10th of December in Stockholm, where the Nobel Laureates receive the Nobel Medal, Diploma, and the prize sum.)

## Are the nominations made public?

The statutes of the Nobel Foundation restrict disclosure of information about the nominations and selecting process for 50 years.

# LITERATURE

Alfred Nobel had broad cultural interests. During his early youth, he developed his literary interests which lasted throughout his life. His library consisted of a rich and broad selection of literature in different languages. During the last years of his life, he tried his hand as an author and began writing fiction. Literature was the fourth prize area Nobel mentioned in his will. The Nobel Prize in Literature is awarded by The Swedish Academy, Stockholm, Sweden.

## About the prize

On 27 November 1895, Alfred Nobel signed his last will and testament, giving the largest share of his fortune to a series of prizes, the Nobel Prizes. As described in Nobel's will one part was dedicated to "the person who shall have produced in the field of literature the most outstanding work in an ideal direction".

**Learn more about the Nobel Prize in Literature from 1901 to 2019.**

| | |
|---|---|
| Nobel Prizes in Literature have been awarded since 1901 | 112 |
| Nobel Prizes in Literature not awarded on Seven occasions | in 1914, 1918, 1935, 1940, 1941, 1942, and 1943. |
| Literature Prizes have been given to one Laureate only. | 108 |
| Literature Prizes have been shared by two Laureates. * | 1904 –Frederic Mistral, Jose Echegaray |

| | |
|---|---|
| | 1917 – Karl Gjellerup, Henrik Pontoppidan<br>1966 –Shmuel Agnon, Nelly Sachs<br>1974 –Evvind Johnson, Harry Martinson |
| Total number of laureates in Literature (1901-2019.) | 116 |
| The youngest Nobel Laureate in Literature | **Rudyard Kipling**<br>**(41 when awarded)** |
| The oldest Nobel Laureate in Literature | **Doris Lessing**<br>**(88 when awarded)** |
| Female Nobel laureates in Literature | 1909 –Selma Lagerlof<br>1926 – Grazia Deledda<br>1928 – Sigrid Undset<br>1938 – Pearl Buck<br>1945 –Gabriela Mistral<br>1966 –Nelly Sachs<br>1991 – Nadine Gordimer<br>1993 – Toni Morrison<br>1996 – Wislawa Szymborska<br>2004 –Elfriede Jelinek<br>2007 – Doris Lessing<br>2009 –Herta Muller<br>2013 –Alice Munro<br>2015 – Svetlana Alexievich<br>2018 –Olga Tokarczuk |
| Multiple Nobel laureates in Literature | No one has been awarded the Nobel Prize in Literature more than once. |
| Two People have declined the Nobel Prize in Literature | **Boris Pasternak**, the 1958 Nobel Prize in Literature, "Accepted first, later caused by the |

<table>
<tr><td></td><td>authorities of his country (Soviet Union) to decline the Prize".<br>Jean Paul Sartre, the 1964 Nobel Prize in Literature, declined the prize because he had consistently declined all official honours.</td></tr>
</table>

***Why is the Literature Prize so seldom divided? The last time was in 1974.**

It probably belongs to the nature of literature. The science prizes are often awarded jointly, as the achievement is jointly, or for doing things that are very close to each other.

## Literature Laureates and languages

Alfred Nobel had an international horizon in his will, though it rejected any consideration for the nationality of the candidates: the worthiest should be chosen, "whether he be Scandinavian or not". The problem of surveying the literature of the whole world was, however, overwhelming and for a long time the Swedish Academy – who selects the Nobel Laureates – was, with justice, to be criticized for making the award a European affair. In 1984, however, the permanent secretary of the Swedish Academy declared that attention to non-European writers was gradually increasing in the Academy; attempts were being made "to achieve a global distribution".

**The 114 Nobel Laureates in Literature from 1901 to 2017 have been writing/writes in the following languages:**

| | | | |
|---|---|---|---|
| English | 29 | Bengali | 1 |
| French | 14 | Chinese | 2 |
| German | 13 | Czech | 1 |
| Spanish | 11 | Finnish | 1 |
| Swedish | 7 | Hebrew | 1 |
| Italian | 6 | Hungarian | 1 |
| Russian | 6 | Icelandic | 1 |
| Polish | 4 | Occitan | 1 |
| Norwegian | 3 | Portuguese | 1 |
| Danish | 3 | Serbo-Croatian | 1 |
| Greek | 2 | Turkish | 1 |
| Japanese | 2 | Yiddish | 1 |
| Arabic | 1 | | |

## Surprise Literature Laureate?

Many believe that Winston Churchill was awarded the Nobel Peace Prize, but he was awarded the 1953 Nobel Prize in Literature. Between 1945 and 1953, Winston Churchill got 21 nominations for the Literature Prize and two for the Nobel Peace Prize.

**The Nobel medal for Literature**

The Nobel medal for Literature was designed by Swedish sculptor and engraver Erik Lindberg and represents a young man sitting under a laurel tree who, enchanted, listens to and writes down the song of the Muse.

# Nominations and selection procedure to the Nobel prize in literature

Nominations to the Nobel prize in literature can be made by qualified persons only. The names of the nominees and other information about the nominations cannot be revealed until 50 years later.

The Nobel Committee for Literature sends invitation letters to persons who are qualified to nominate for the Nobel Prize in Literature.

**The Swedish Academy** is responsible for the selection of the Nobel Laureates in Literature and has 18 members. The Nobel Committee for Literature is the working body that evaluates the nominations and presents its recommendations to the Swedish Academy and comprises four to five members.

The candidates eligible for the Literature Prize are those nominated by qualified persons who have received an invitation from the Nobel Committee to submit names for consideration. Other persons who are qualified to nominate but have not received invitations may also submit nominations. No one can nominate himself or herself.

How are the Nobel Laureates in Literature selected?

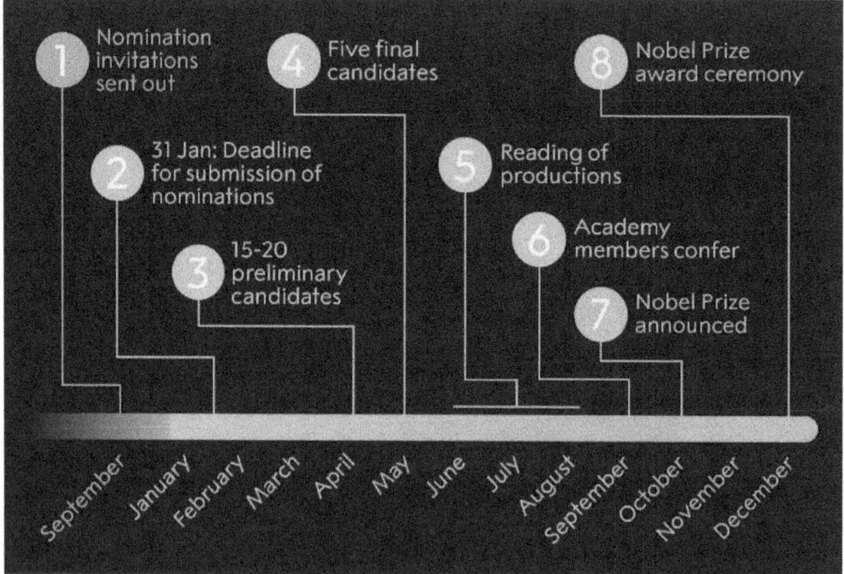


The nomination process for Nobel Laureates in Literature Ill. N. Elmehed

**Below is a brief description of the process involved in choosing the Nobel Laureates in Literature**.

**September** – *Invitation letters are sent out.*

(The Nobel Committee sends out nomination forms to hundreds of individuals and organizations qualified to nominate for the Nobel Prize in Literature.)

**February** – *Deadline for submission.*

(The completed forms must reach the Nobel Committee not later than 31 January of the following year. The Committee then screens the nominations and submits a list for approval by the Academy.)

**April** – *Preliminary candidates.*

(After further studies, the Committee selects 15–20 names for consideration as preliminary candidates by the Academy.)

**May** – *Final candidates.*

(The Committee whittles down the list to five priority candidates to be considered by the Academy.)

**June-August** – *Reading of productions.*

(The members of the Academy read and assess the work of the final candidates during the summer. The Nobel Committee also prepares individual reports.)

**September** – *Academy members confer.*

(Having read the work of the final candidates, members of the Academy discuss the merits of the different candidates' contribution.)

**October** – *Nobel Laureates are chosen.*

(In early October, the Academy chooses the Nobel Laureate in Literature. A candidate must receive more than half of the votes cast. The Nobel Laureates names are then announced.)

**December** – *Nobel Laureates receive their prize.*

(The Nobel Prize Award Ceremony takes place on 10 December in Stockholm, where the Nobel Laureates receive their Nobel Prize, which consists of a Nobel Medal and Diploma, and a document confirming the prize amount.)

## Are the nominations made public?

The statutes of the Nobel Foundation restrict disclosure of information about the nominations, whether publicly or privately, for 50 years. The restriction concerns the nominees and nominators, as well as investigations and opinions related to the award of a prize.

# PEACE

Alfred Nobel showed a big interest in social issues and was engaged in the peace movement. His acquaintance with Bertha von Suttner, who was a driving force in the international peace movement in Europe and later awarded the Peace Prize, influenced his views on peace. Peace was the fifth and final prize area that Nobel mentioned in his will. The Nobel Peace Prize is awarded by a committee elected by the Norwegian Parliament (Stortinget).

## About the prize:

On 27 November 1895, Alfred Nobel signed his last will and testament, giving the largest share of his fortune to a series of prizes, the Nobel Prizes. As described in Nobel's will, one part was dedicated to "the person who shall have done the most or the best work for fraternity between nations, for the abolition or reduction of standing armies and for the holding and promotion of peace congresses".

**Learn more about the Nobel Peace Prize from 1901 to 2019.**

| | |
|---|---|
| Nobel Prizes in Peace have been awarded since 1901 | 100 |
| Nobel Prizes in Peace not awarded on nineteen occasions | in 1914-1916, 1918, 1923, 1924, 1928, 1932, 1939-1943, 1948, 1955-1956, 1966-1967 and 1972. |
| Peace Prizes have been given to one Laureate only. | 68 |
| Peace Prizes have been shared by two Laureates. | 30 |

| | |
|---|---|
| Peace Prizes have been shared between three Laureates. | 2 |
| Total number of laureates in Peace (1901-2019.) | 134* (107 individuals and 27 organizations.) |
| The youngest Nobel Laureate in Peace | **Malala Yousafzai (17 when awarded)** |
| The oldest Nobel Laureate in Peace | Joseph Rotblat (87 when awarded) |
| Female Nobel laureates in Peace | 1905 –Bertha von Suttner<br>1931 –Jane Addams<br>1946 –Emily Greene Balch<br>1976 –Betty Williams<br>1976 –Mairead Corrigan<br>1979 – Mother Teresa<br>1982 – Alva Myrdal<br>1991 – Aung San Suu Kyi<br>1992 – Rigoberta Menchu Tum<br>1997 –Jody Williams<br>2003 – Shirin Ebadi<br>2004 – Wangari Maathai<br>2011 – Ellen Johnson Sirleaf<br>2011 – Leymah Gbowee<br>2011 – Tawkkol Karman<br>2014 –Malal Yousafzai<br>2018 –Nadia Murad |
| Multiple Nobel laureates in Peace | International Committee of the Red Cross (ICRC) has been honored the most – three times 1917, 1944 and 1963 |

| | |
|---|---|
| | Linus Pauling - in Chemistry 1954 and in Peace 1962<br><br>United Nations High Commissioner for Refugees (UNHCR) 1954 and 1981 |
| Peace Prize Laureate declined the Nobel Peace Prize | Le Duc Tho The Vietnamese politician awarded the 1973 Nobel Peace Prize jointly with US Secretary of State Henry Kissinger, is the only person who has declined the Nobel Peace Prize. |
| Nobel Peace Prize Laureates under arrest at the time of the award | Carl von Ossietzky German pacifist and journalist<br>Aung San Suu Kyi Burmese politician<br>Liu Xiaobo Chinese human rights activist |

*Since Comité International de la Croix Rouge (International Committee of the Red Cross) was awarded three times and Office of the United Nations High Commissioner for Refugees was awarded twice there are **107** individuals and **24** organizations that have been awarded the Nobel Peace Prize.

## Surprise Nobel Peace Prize Laureate?

Many believe that, Winston Churchill was awarded the Nobel Peace Prize, but he was awarded the 1953 Nobel Prize in Literature. In fact, Churchill was nominated both for the Literature Prize and for the Nobel Peace Prize.

# Nominated but not awarded

The three most common searches on individuals in the Nobel Peace Prize nomination database are Adolf Hitler, Mahatma Gandhi and Joseph Stalin.

- ➤ **Joseph Stalin**, the Secretary General of the Communist Party of the Soviet Union (1922-1953), was nominated for the Nobel Peace Prize in 1945 and 1948 for his efforts to end World War II.

- ➤ **Mahatma Gandhi**, one of the strongest symbols of non-violence in the 20th century, was nominated in 1937, 1938, 1939, 1947 and, finally, shortly before he was assassinated in January 1948. Although Gandhi was not awarded the Prize (a posthumous award is not allowed by the statutes), the Norwegian Nobel Committee decided to make no award that year on the grounds that "there was no suitable living candidate".

- ➤ **Adolf Hitler** was nominated once in 1939. As unlikely as it may seem today, Adolf Hitler was nominated for the Nobel Peace Prize in 1939 by a member of the Swedish parliament, E.G.C. Brandt. Apparently, Brandt never intended the nomination to be taken seriously. Brandt was a dedicated antifascist and had intended this nomination more as a satiric criticism of the current political debate in Sweden. At the time, several Swedish parliamentarians had nominated then British Prime Minister Neville Chamberlin for the Nobel Peace Prize, a nomination which Brandt viewed with great skepticism. However, Brandt's satirical intentions were not well received, and the nomination was swiftly withdrawn in a letter dated 1 February 1939.

## Other statesmen and national leaders who were nominated but not awarded the Nobel Peace Prize:

- *Czechoslovakia:* Thomas G. Masaryk, Edvard Benes,
- *Great Britain:* Neville Chamberlain, Anthony Eden, Clement Attlee,Ramsay MacDonald, Winston Churchill
- *USA:* the presidents William Howard Taft, Warren G. Harding, Herbert Hoover, Franklin D. Roosevelt, Harry S. Truman & Dwight D. Eisenhower; the foreign ministers Charles Hughes, John Foster Dulles
- *France:* Pierre Mendès-France
- *Western Germany:* Konrad Adenauer
- *Argentina:* Juan and Eva Peron
- *India:* Mahatma Gandhi, Jawaharlal Nehru
- *Finland:* Juho Kusti Paasikivi
- *Italy:* Benito Mussolini

## Artists nominated but not awarded the Peace Prize:

- **Leo Tolstoy** (Russian author),
- **E.M. Remarque** (German author),
- **Pablo Casals** (Spanish Catalan cellist and later conductor),
- **Nicholas Roerich**.

## Nominees not primarily known for their peace work:

- **John Maynard Keynes**, British economist.
- **Pierre de Coubertin**, French pedagogue and historian best

known for founding the International Olympic Committee.

> **Lord Baden-Powell**, Lieutenant-General in the British Army, writer, founder of the Scout Movement.

> **Maria Montessori**, best known for her philosophy and method of educating children from birth to adolescence. Her educational method is still in use today in a number of public as well as private schools throughout the world.

## Royal nominees:

> **Tsar Nikolai II** (1901),

> **Prince Carl of Sweden** (1919),

> **King Albert I of Belgium** (1922),

> **Emperor Haile Selassi of Ethiopia** (1938),

> **King Paul I of Greece** (1950),

> **Princess Wilhelmina of the Netherlands** (1951).

## How many times can someone be nominated?

Jane Addams was nominated 91 times between 1916 and 1931, when she was finally awarded the Nobel Peace Prize. By contrast Emily Green Balch, Fridtjof Nansen and Theodore Roosevelt received the Nobel Peace Prize the first year that they were nominated.

# Why a Norwegian committee for the Nobel Peace Prize?

All Nobel Prizes are awarded in Stockholm, Sweden, except for the Nobel Peace Prize, which is awarded in Oslo, Norway. The founder of the Nobel Prize, Alfred Nobel, was a Swedish cosmopolitan. In his will, he declared that the Nobel Peace Prize should be awarded by a Norwegian committee. When Alfred Nobel was alive, Norway and Sweden were united under one monarch, until 1905 when Norway became an independent kingdom.

## The Nobel Peace Prize medal

The Nobel Peace Prize medal was designed by Norwegian sculptor Gustav Vigeland and shows Alfred Nobel in a pose slightly different from that of the other medals.

# Nominations and selection procedure to the Nobel prize in peace

A nomination for the Nobel Peace Prize may be submitted by any person who meets the nomination criteria. A letter of invitation to submit is not required. The names of the nominees and other information about the nominations cannot be revealed until 50 years later.

### 2020 Nobel Peace Prize nominations

There are 318 candidates for the Nobel Peace Prize for 2020, of which 211 are individuals and 107 are organizations.

318 is the fourth highest number of candidates ever. The current record of 376 candidates was reached in 2016.

Neither the names of nominators nor of nominees for the Nobel Peace Prize may be divulged until 50 years have elapsed.

## Process of nomination and selection

The Norweian Nobel Committee is responsible for selecting the Nobel Peace Prize Laureates. A nomination for the Nobel Peace Prize may be submitted by any persons who are qualified to nominate.

## Qualified nominators

According to the statutes of the Nobel Foundation, a nomination is considered valid if it is submitted by a person who falls within one of the following categories:

- Members of national assemblies and national governments (cabinet members/ministers) of sovereign states as well as current heads of states
- Members of The International Court of Justice in The Hague and The Permanent Court of Arbitration in The Hague
- Members of l'Institut de Droit International
- Members of the international board of the Women's International League for Peace and Freedom
- University professors, professors emeriti and associate professors of history, social sciences, law, philosophy, theology, and religion; university rectors and university directors (or their equivalents); directors of peace research institutes and foreign policy institutes
- Persons who have been awarded the Nobel Peace Prize
- Members of the main board of directors or its equivalent of organizations that have been awarded the Nobel Peace Prize
- Current and former members of the Norwegian Nobel Committee (proposals by current members of the Committee

to be submitted no later than at the first meeting of the Committee after 1 February)
- ➢ Former advisers to the Norwegian Nobel Committee

Unless otherwise stated the term members shall be understood as current (sitting) members.

## Candidacy criteria

The candidates eligible for the Nobel Peace Prize are those persons or organizations nominated by qualified individuals, see above. A nomination for yourself will not be taken into consideration.

## Selection of Nobel Laureates

The Norwegian Nobel Committee is responsible for the selection of eligible candidates and the choice of the Nobel Peace Prize Laureates. The Committee is composed of five members appointed by the Storting (Norwegian parliament). The Nobel Peace Prize is awarded in Oslo, Norway, not in Stockholm, Sweden, where the Nobel Prizes in Physics, Chemistry, Physiology or Medicine, Literature and the Economics Prize are awarded.

## How are the Nobel Laureates selected?

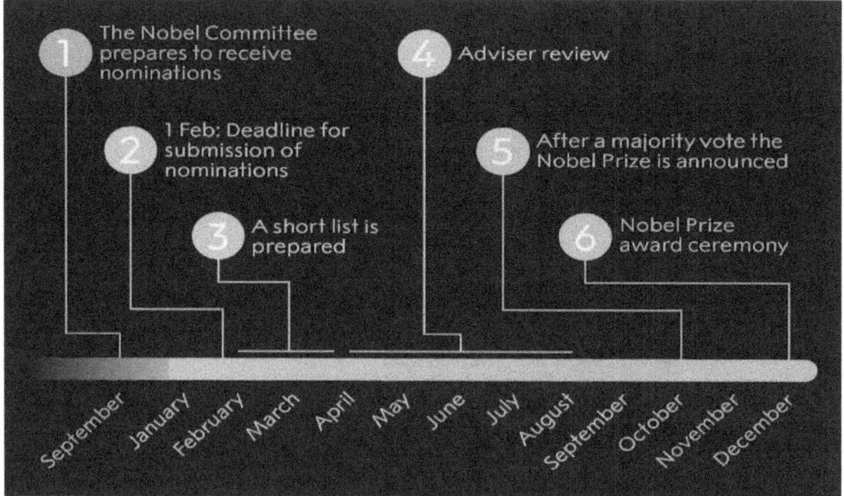


The nomination process for Nobel Peace Prize Laureates Ill. N. Elmehed

**Below is a brief description of the process involved in selecting the Nobel Peace Prize Laureates.**

**September** – *The Norwegian Nobel Committee prepares to receive nominations.*

( These nominations will be submitted by members of national assemblies, governments, and international courts of law; university chancellors, professors of social science, history, philosophy, law and theology; leaders of peace research institutes and institutes of foreign affairs; previous Nobel Peace Prize Laureates; board members of organizations that have received the Nobel Peace Prize; present and past members of the Norwegian Nobel Committee; and former advisers of the Norwegian Nobel Institute.)

**February** – *Deadline for submission.*

(In order to be considered for the award of the year, nominations for the Nobel Peace Prize shall be sent into the Norwegian Nobel Committee in Oslo before the 1st day of February the same year. Nominations postmarked and received after this date are included in the following year's discussions. In recent years, the Committee has received close to 200 different nominations for different nominations for the Nobel Peace Prize. The number of nominating letters is much higher, as many are for the same candidates.)

**February-March** – *Short list.*

(The Committee assesses the candidates' work and prepares a short list.)

**March-August** – *Adviser review.*

**October** – *Nobel Laureates are chosen.*

(At the beginning of October, the Nobel Committee chooses the Nobel Peace Prize Laureates through a majority vote. The decision is final and without appeal. The names of the Nobel Peace Prize Laureates are then announced.)

**December** – *Nobel Laureates receive their prize.*

(The Nobel Peace Prize Award Ceremony takes place on 10 December in Oslo, Norway, where the Nobel Laureates receive their Nobel Prize, which consists of a Nobel Medal and Diploma, and a document confirming the prize amount.)

## Are the nominations made public?

The statutes of the Nobel Foundation restrict disclosure of information about the nominations, whether publicly or privately, for 50 years. The restriction concerns the nominees and nominators, as well as investigations and opinions related to the award of a prize.

# Submission

## Submission of nominations

The Norwegian Nobel Committee has launched an on-line nomination form that you can use if you are a qualified nominator (see the list 'Qualified nominators') above). The form can be reached from the website of the Norwegian Nobel Committee between September and February.

## Deadline for nominations

Nomination deadline is 31 January at 12 midnight CET. Nominations which do not meet the deadline are normally included in the following year's assessment. Members of the Nobel Committee are entitled to submit their own nominations as late as at the first meeting of the Committee after the expiry of the deadline.

## Submission confirmation

A letter or e-mail confirming the receipt of the submitted nomination is normally sent out within a couple of months of the submission deadline.

## Selection process

At the first meeting of the Nobel Committee after the February 1 deadline for nominations, the Committee's Permanent Secretary presents the list of the year's candidates. The Committee may on that occasion add further names to the list, after which the nomination process is closed, and discussion of the particular candidates begins. In the light of this first review, the Committee draws up the so-called short list – i.e. the list of candidates selected for more thorough consideration. The short list typically contains from twenty to thirty candidates.

The candidates on the short list are then considered by the Nobel Institute's permanent advisers. In addition to the Institute's Director and Research Director, the body of advisers generally consists of a small group of Norwegian university professors with broad expertise in subject areas with a bearing on the Peace Prize. The advisers usually have a couple of months in which to draw up their reports. Reports are also occasionally requested from other Norwegian and foreign experts.

When the advisers' reports have been presented, the Nobel Committee embarks on a thorough-going discussion of the most likely candidates. In the process, the need often arises to obtain additional information and updates about candidates from additional experts, often foreign. As a rule, the Committee reaches a decision only at its very last meeting before the announcement of the Prize at the beginning of October.

The Committee seeks to achieve unanimity in its selection of the Peace Prize Laureate. On the rare occasions when this proves impossible, the selection is decided by a simple majority vote.

## 50-year secrecy rule

The Committee does not itself announce the names of nominees, neither to the media nor to the candidates themselves. In so far as certain names crop up in the advance speculations as to who will be awarded any given year's Prize, this is either sheer guesswork or information put out by the person or persons behind the nomination. Information in the Nobel Committee's nomination database is not made public until after fifty years.

# ECONOMIC SCIENCE

In 1968, Sveriges Riksbank (Sweden's central bank) established the Prize in Economic Sciences in Memory of Alfred Nobel, founder of the Nobel Prize. The Prize is based on a donation received by the Nobel Foundation in 1968 from Sveriges Riksbank on the Bank's 300th anniversary. The first Prize in Economic Sciences was awarded to Ragnar Frisch and Jan Tinbergen in 1969.

The Prize in Economic Sciences is awarded by The Royal Swedish Academy of Sciences, Stockholm, Sweden, according to the same principles as for the Nobel Prizes that have been awarded since 1901.

**Learn more about the Sveriges Riksbank Prize in Economic Sciences in Memory of Alfred Nobel, awarded from 1969 to 2019.**

| | |
|---|---|
| Nobel Prizes in Economic Sciences have been awarded since 1969 | 51 |
| Economic Sciences Prizes have been given to one Laureate only. | 25 |
| Economic Sciences Prizes have been shared by two Laureates. | 19 |
| Economic Sciences Prizes have been shared between three Laureates. | 7 |
| Total number of laureates in Economic Sciences (1969-2019.) | 84 |

| The youngest Nobel Laureate in Economic Sciences | Esther Duflo (46 when awarded) |
|---|---|
| The oldest Nobel Laureate in Economic Sciences | Leonid Hurwicz (90 when awarded) |
| Female Nobel laureates in Economic Sciences | Elinor Ostrom - 2009. Esther Duflo - 2019 |
| Multiple Nobel laureates in Economic Sciences | So far there are no multiple Laureates in Economic Sciences. |
| Couple laureates in Economic Sciences | Gunnar Myrdal (Economic Sciences in 1974) and Alva Myrdal (Nobel Peace Prize in 1982) |
| Brother laureates in Economic Sciences | Jan Tinbergen (Economic Sciences in 1969) and Nikolaas Tinbergen (Physiology or Medicine in 1973) |

## The medal for the Prize in Economic Sciences

The medal for Economic Sciences was designed by Swedish artist and sculptor Gunvor Svensson-Lundqvist and shows the North Star emblem of the Royal Swedish Academy of Sciences.

## Nomination and selection procedure to the   prize in economic sciences

Nomination to the prize in economic sciences is by invitation only. The names of the nominees and other information about the nominations cannot be revealed until 50 years later.

The Economic Sciences Prize Committee sends confidential forms to persons who are competent and qualified to nominate.

**The Royal Swedish Academy of Sciences** is responsible for the selection of the Laureates in Economic Sciences from among the candidates recommended by the Economic Sciences Prize Committee. The Committee is the working body that screens the nominations and selects the final candidates. It consists of five members, but for many years the Committee has included adjunct members with the same voting rights as members.

The candidates eligible for the Prize in Economic Sciences are those nominated by qualified persons who have received an invitation from the Economic Sciences Prize Committee to submit names for consideration. No one can nominate himself or herself.

How are the laureates in economic sciences selected?

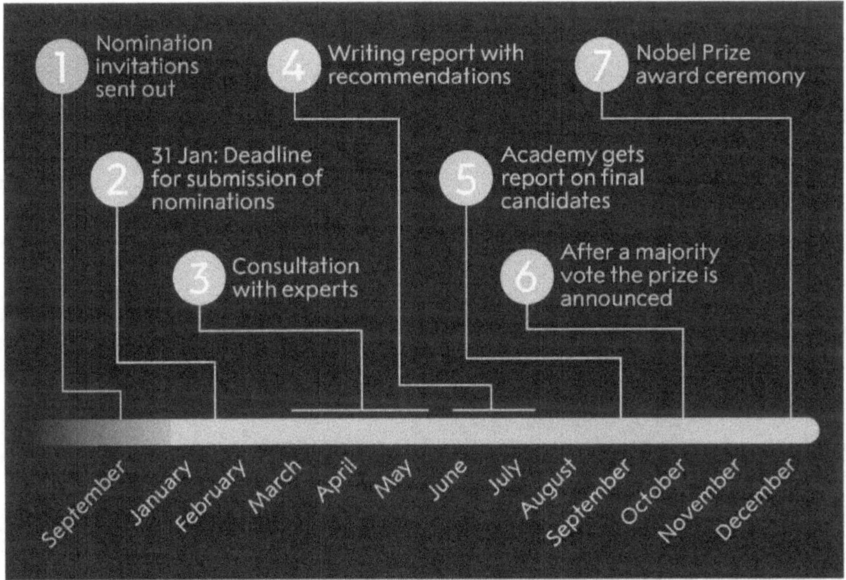


The nomination process for Laureates in Economic Sciences Ill. N. Elmehed

**Below is a brief description of the process involved in choosing the Laureates in Economic Sciences.**

**September** – *Nomination forms are sent out.*

(The Economic Sciences Prize Committee sends out confidential forms to around 3,000 individuals – selected professors at universities around the world, Laureates in Economic Sciences, and members of the Royal Swedish Academy of Sciences, among others.)

**February** – *Deadline for submission.*

(The completed forms must reach the Economic Sciences Prize Committee no later than January 31 of the following year. The Committee screens the nominations and selects the preliminary candidates. About 250-350 names are nominated as the same names are often submitted by several nominators.)

**March-May** – *Consultation with experts.*

(The Economic Sciences Prize Committee sends the names of the preliminary candidates to specially appointed experts for their assessment of the candidates' work.)

**June-August** – *Writing of the report.*

(The Economic Sciences Prize Committee puts together the report with recommendations to be submitted to the Academy. The report is signed by all members of the Committee.)

**September** – *Committee submits recommendations.*

(The Economic Sciences Prize Committee submits its report with recommendations on the final candidates to the members of the Academy. The report is discussed at two meetings of the Economic Sciences Section of the Academy.)

**October** – *Economic Sciences Laureates are chosen.*

(In early October, the Academy of Sciences selects the Laureates in Economic Sciences through a majority vote. The decision is final and without appeal. The names of the Laureates in Economic Sciences are then announced.)

**December** – *Economic Sciences Laureates receive their prize.*

(The Nobel Prize Award Ceremony takes place on 10 December in Stockholm, where the Nobel Laureates receive their Nobel Prize, which consists of a Nobel Medal and Diploma, and a document confirming the prize amount.)

## Are the nominations made public?

The statutes of the Nobel Foundation restrict disclosure of information about the nominations, whether publicly or privately, for 50 years. The restriction concerns the nominees and nominators, as well as investigations and opinions related to the award of a prize.

## Not a Nobel Prize

The Prize in Economic Sciences is not a Nobel Prize. In 1968, Sveriges Riksbank (Sweden's central bank) instituted "The Sveriges Riksbank Prize in Economic Sciences in Memory of Alfred Nobel", and it has since been awarded by the Royal Swedish Academy of Sciences according to the same principles as for the Nobel Prizes that have been awarded since 1901. The first Prize in Economic Sciences was awarded to Ragnar Frisch and Jan Tinbergen in 1969.

# NOBEL PRIZE AWARD CEREMONIES

Overview of the Nobel Prize award ceremony.© Nobel Media. Photo: Alexander Mahmoud

### 10 December - A magic date

Since 1901, the Nobel Prizes have been presented to Nobel Laureates at ceremonies on 10 December, the anniversary of Alfred Nobel's death.

As stipulated in Nobel's will, the Nobel Prizes in Physics, Chemistry, Physiology or Medicine and Literature are awarded in Stockholm, Sweden, while the Nobel Peace Prize is awarded in Oslo, Norway.

Since 1969 an additional prize has been awarded at the ceremony in Stockholm - the Sveriges Riksbank Prize in Economic Sciences in Memory of Alfred Nobel.

# Facts

- In Stockholm laureates receive the Nobel Prize medal and diploma from King Carl XVI Gustaf of Sweden.

- In Oslo laureates receive the Nobel Peace Prize from the Chairman of the Norwegian Nobel Committee in the presence of King Harald V of Norway.

- Every laureate is expected to deliver a lecture in order to receive their prize.

- The Nobel Banquet is held every year on 10 December to celebrate the year's Nobel Laureates. Each Banquet has included a unique menu for the guests. 1,300 guests can be seated in the Blue Hall of the City Hall of Stockholm where the banquet has been held since 1934.

- For most people, attending the Nobel Prize banquet or award ceremony is a once in a lifetime experience – and one with a strict dress code.

- Male guests have an even stricter dress code. Many Nobel Laureates make a trip to Hans Allde, a Stockholm-based outfitter, for the white tie and tails required for both the award ceremony and banquet.

# THE NOBEL PRIZE ORGANISATION

Alfred Nobel had a vision of a better world. He believed that people are capable of helping to improve society through knowledge, science and humanism. This is why he created a prize that would reward the discoveries that have conferred the greatest benefit to humankind. Since 1901, the Nobel Prize has been awarded in the fields of physics, chemistry, physiology or medicine, literature and peace, while a memorial prize in economic sciences was added in 1968.

The economic foundations for the Nobel Prize were laid in 1895, when Alfred Nobel signed his last will and left much of his wealth to the establishment of a prize and the subsequent Nobel Foundation, which is tasked with a mission to manage his fortune and has ultimate responsibility for fulfilling the intentions of Nobel's will. In accordance with the instructions Nobel left through his will, various independent prize-awarding institutions have selected Nobel Laureates in each prize category for more than a century.

Today, there are also several outreach organisations and activities that have been developed to inspire generations and disseminate knowledge about the Nobel Prize through events, exhibitions, educational efforts, and digital outreach.

## The Nobel foundation

The Nobel foundation has ultimate responsibility for fulfilling the intentions in Alfred Nobel's will.

The Nobel Foundation, a private institution established in 1900, has ultimate responsibility for fulfilling the intentions in Alfred Nobel's will. The main mission of the Nobel Foundation is to manage Alfred Nobel's fortune in a manner that ensures a secure financial standing for the Nobel Prize over the long term and that the prize-awarding institutions are guaranteed independence in their work of selecting recipients.

The Foundation is also tasked with strengthening the Nobel Prize's position by administering and developing the brands and intangible assets that have been built up during the Nobel Prize's history, which spans more than 100 years.

The Nobel Foundation also strives to safeguard the prize-awarding institutions' common interests and to represent the Nobel organisation. In the past two decades several outreach activities have been developed with the aim of inspiring and disseminating knowledge about the Nobel Prize.

## The Nobel Prize awarding institutions

Who selects the Nobel Laureates?
In his last will and testament, Alfred Nobel specifically designated the institutions responsible for the prizes he wished to be established: The Royal Swedish Academy of Sciences for the Nobel Prize in Physics and Chemistry, Karolinska Institutet for the Nobel Prize in Physiology or Medicine, the Swedish Academy for the Nobel Prize in Literature, and a Committee of five persons to be elected by the Norwegian Parliament (Storting) for the Nobel Peace Prize.

In 1968, the Sveriges Riksbank established the Sveriges Riksbank Prize in Economic Sciences in Memory of Alfred Nobel. The Royal Swedish Academy of Sciences was given the task to select the Laureates in Economic Sciences starting in 1969.

## List of the prize awarding institutions

> ➤ The Royal Swedish Academy of Sciences

> ➤ The Nobel Assembly of Karolinska Institutet

> ➤ The Swedish Academy

> ➤ The Norwegian Nobel Committee

# Financial Management

On 27 November 1895, a year before his death, Alfred Nobel signed the famous Will which would implement some of the goals to which he had devoted so much of his life. Nobel stipulated in his will that most of his estate, more than SEK 31 million (today approximately SEK 1,794 million) should be converted into a fund and invested in "safe securities".

The income from the investments was to be "distributed annually in the form of prizes to those who during the preceding year have conferred the greatest benefit on humankind."

The Nobel Foundation is a private institution established in 1900 based on the will. The investment policy of the Foundation is naturally of paramount importance to the preservation and, if possible, the augmentation of the funds and, thus, of the prize amount. According to the original 1901 investment rules, the term "safe securities" was, in the spirit of that time, interpreted to mean gilt-edged bonds or loans backed by such securities or backed by mortgages on real estate. With the changes brought about by the two World Wars and their economic and financial aftermath, the term "safe securities" had to be reinterpreted in the light of prevailing economic conditions and tendencies. Thus, at the request of the

Foundation's Board of Directors, in the early 1950s the Swedish Government sanctioned changes, whereby the board for all practical purposes was given a free hand to invest not only in real estate, bonds and secured loans, but also in most types of stocks.

From 1901, when the first prizes (SEK 150,000 each) were awarded, the prize amounts declined steadily. But with this freedom to invest, along with the long-fought-for tax-exemption granted in 1946, it was possible to reverse this trend and, on average, even keep pace with increasing inflation. The real value of the prize amount in SEK terms was finally restored in 1991. The amount of the 2019 Nobel Prize is set to SEK 9.0 million.

# ANNEXURE I

Updated 2020-02-03

## Board of Directors: Regular members

- Professor Carl-Henrik Heldin, Chairman
- Professor Göran K. Hansson, Vice Chairman
  *Secretary General of the Royal Swedish Academy of Sciences*
- Dr Lars Heikensten,
  *Executive Director*
- Professor Mats Malm
  *Permanent Secretary of the Swedish Academy*
- Mr Tomas Nicolin, MSc
- Professor Thomas Perlmann
  *Secretary of the Nobel Assembly at Karolinska Institutet and of the Nobel Committee for Physiology or Medicine*
- Mrs Berit Reiss-Andersen
  *Chair Of The Norwegian Nobel Committee*

### Deputy members

- Professor Gunnar von Heijne
  *Secretary of the Nobel Committee for Chemistry*
- Professor Gunnar Ingelman
  *Secretary of the Nobel Committee for Physics*

## Trustees of the Nobel Foundation

- Sven Lidin, Chairman

# Elected by the Royal Swedish Academy of Sciences

- Olga Botner
- Martin Jakobsson
- Siv Andersson
- Sven Lidin
- Dan Larhammar
- Per Delsing

## Deputy Trustees

- Kerstin Sahlin
- Kerstin Lidén
- Olle Inganäs
- Anne L'Huillier

# Elected by the Nobel Assembly at Karolinska Institutet

- Christer Höög
- Jesper Haeggström
- Anna Wedell

## Deputy Trustees

- Nils-Göran Larsson
- Gunilla Karlsson Hedestam

# Elected by the Swedish Academy

- Ellen Mattson
- Eric M. Runesson

## Deputy Trustees

- Anders Olsson
- Anne Swärd

# Elected by the Norwegian Nobel Committee

- Anne Enger
- Asle Toje
- Henrik Syse

## Deputy Trustees

- Thorbjørn Jagland
- Olav Njølstad

# Auditors

- Dr Jonas Björck, Chairman,

  appointed by the Swedish Government
- Mr Jonas Svensson, Authorized Public Accountant,

  elected by the Trustees of the Nobel Foundation
- Professor Lars Bergström,

  elected by the Royal Swedish Academy of Sciences
- Professor Catharina Larsson,

  elected by the Nobel Assembly at Karolinska Institutet

- Professor Tomas Riad,

  elected by the Swedish Academy

- Bettina Banoun,

  elected by the Norwegian Nobel Committee

# ANNEXURE II

## POEM 118 – THE NOBEL MUSEUM

*Posted on <u>April 24, 2013</u> by <u>The Hapless Neo-Romantic</u> under <u>Stockholm</u>*

### You say I am a riddle

You say I am a riddle – it may be

For all of us are riddles unexplained.

Begun in pain, in deeper torture ended,

This breathing clay what business has it here?

Some petty wants to chain us to the Earth,

Some lofty thoughts to lift us to the spheres,

And cheat us with that semblance of a soul

To dream of Immortality, till Time

O'er empty visions draws the closing veil,

And a new life begins – the life of worms,

Those hungry plunderers of the human breast.

For this Hope dwindles as we fathom Truth:

Forgotten to forget – and is that all?

To-day a man, with power to act and feel,

A mirror of the Universe, wherein

Creation's centred rays combine to form

The focus of Intelligence; to-day

A heart so deeply loving that it seems

As if that band uniting soul to soul,

Were but Religion in a brighter form;

To-day all this – to-morrow a cold corpse,

A something worse than clay which stinks and rots.

Kind hands may strew their flowers,

kind eyes may drop

A tear of pity o'er the buried dust;

But worms will feed long after friends are gone,

And, after all, what matters love of theirs

When all of us, that was, is at an end.

– Alfred Nobel

# REFERENCES

1.  Alfred Nobel and His Interest in Literature. NobelPrize.org.
    Nobel Media AB 2019. Wed. 23 Oct 2019.
    <https://www.nobelprize.org/alfred-nobel/alfred-nobel-and-
    his-interest-in-literature/>

2.  Alfred Nobel's health and his interest in medicine.
    NobelPrize.org. Nobel Media AB 2019. Wed. 23 Oct 2019.
    <https://www.nobelprize.org/alfred-nobel/alfred-nobels-
    health-and-his-interest-in-medicine/>

3.  Alfred Nobel's life and work. NobelPrize.org. Nobel Media
    AB 2019. Wed. 23 Oct 2019.
    <https://www.nobelprize.org/alfred-nobel/alfred-nobels-
    life-and-work/>

4.  Alfred Nobel – Life and Philosophy. NobelPrize.org. Nobel
    Media AB 2019. Wed. 23 Oct 2019.
    <https://www.nobelprize.org/alfred-nobel/alfred-nobel-life-
    and-philosophy/>

5.  Alfred Nobel – St. Petersburg, 1842-1863. NobelPrize.org.
    Nobel Media AB 2019. Wed. 23 Oct 2019.
    <https://www.nobelprize.org/alfred-nobel/alfred-nobel-st-
    petersburg-1842-1863/>

6.  Alfred Nobel – the poet. NobelPrize.org. Nobel Media AB
    2019. Wed. 23 Oct 2019.
    <https://www.nobelprize.org/alfred-nobel/alfred-nobel-the-
    poet/>

7.  Alfred Nobel's Thoughts about War and Peace.
    NobelPrize.org. Nobel Media AB 2019. Wed. 23 Oct 2019.

https://www.nobelprize.org/alfred-nobel/alfred-nobels-thoughts-about-war-and-peace/

8. Auditors. NobelPrize.org. Nobel Media AB 2020. Mon. 13 Apr 2020. <https://www.nobelprize.org/about/auditors/>

9. Board of directors. NobelPrize.org. Nobel Media AB 2020. Mon. 13 Apr 2020. <https://www.nobelprize.org/about/board-of-directors/>

10. Erlandsson, Åke, Alfred Nobel's Private Library, Björkborn, Nobelprize.org.

11. Financial management. NobelPrize.org. Nobel Media AB 2020. Mon. 13 Apr 2020. https://www.nobelprize.org/about/financial-management/

12. Nobel Symposia. NobelPrize.org. Nobel Media AB 2020. Mon. 13 Apr 2020. <https://www.nobelprize.org/about/nobel-symposia/>

13. Nomination and selection of Laureates in Economic Sciences. NobelPrize.org. Nobel Media AB 2019. Thu. 31 Oct 2019. <https://www.nobelprize.org/nomination/economic-sciences/>

14. Nomination and selection of Literature Laureates. NobelPrize.org. Nobel Media AB 2019. Thu. 31 Oct 2019. <https://www.nobelprize.org/nomination/literature/>

15. Nomination and selection of Peace Prize Laureates. NobelPrize.org. Nobel Media AB 2020. Mon. 13 Apr 2020. <https://www.nobelprize.org/nomination/peace/>

16. Sjöman, Vilgot, Vem älskar Alfred Nobel? Stockholm, 2001. Suttner, Bertha von, Memoiren. Stuttgart, 1909.

17. Statutes of the Nobel Foundation. NobelPrize.org. Nobel Media AB 2020. Mon. 13 Apr 2020. <https://www.nobelprize.org/about/statutes-of-the-nobel-foundation/>

18. https://thehaplessneoromantic.wordpress.com/2013/04/24/poem-118-the-nobel-museum/

19. Trustees. NobelPrize.org. Nobel Media AB 2020. Mon. 13 Apr 2020. https://www.nobelprize.org/about/trustees/

20. http://nobelmuseetikarlskoga.se/index.php/home)

# ABOUT THE AUTHOR

Hi, I am Sonali Dorge-Phule born and raised in Pune, India. I reside in South Korea with my husband and little princess. I am wife, mother, and Librarian by profession. I began my writing with a poetry book in Marathi language- Kavita Manatlya. In my spare time I love to read, cook, dance, write and garden.

Since from my childhood Nobel Prize always fascinate me! To read about scientist and their dynamic inventions was pleasing experience for me. It is my pleasure that I got this opportunity to write about Nobel prize and all Nobel winners. This is my first nonfiction book. Let's share stories of Nobel people from all over the world. I am sure, it will be a great experience for you.